LAMBS

THE UMPIRES
'He just walked up to r̶...
mucked up this Test for you', and then just walked on.
I didn't know what to say. I just looked at him and felt so sorry for the bloke.'

HIS BATSMEN
'I was disgusted at their lack of resistance and let them know before we went out to bowl. They had to redeem themselves.'

WINNING
'I had a special reason to smile. Besides recording my first victory as Australian captain, I had inflicted Mike Brearley's first defeat in sixteen Tests at the England helm.'

LOSING
'We were distressed at our performance. I was disgusted. Seven of our last eight batsmen contributed a paltry nine runs between us.'

HOGG
'Nobody will ever do that to me again!'

COLLAPSING
'In just one hour we had lost 6-15, the Test, hopes of squaring the series, regaining lost honour from Sydney, and all confidence.'

LAMBS TO THE SLAUGHTER
Graham Yallop

NEW ENGLISH LIBRARY/TIMES MIRROR

First published in Australia by
Outback Press Pty Ltd in 1979
© 1979 by Graham Yallop

First NEL paperback edition December 1980

NEL Books are published by
New English Library Limited,
Barnard's Inn, Holborn,
London EC1N 2JR.
Printed and bound in Great Britain by
Collins, Glasgow

45004774 1

Contents

1 Sacked

I was captain of my country and a lifelong dream was a reality ... but just a few turbulent months later that dream was shattered in a nightmare summer.

From go to whoa I was on the receiving end: England handed Australia a 5–1 drubbing in the harshest defeat recorded in more than 100 years of Ashes battle; I captained the side to six losses in seven Tests; I was injured for the final Test victory of the summer; and then, crunch!

I was sacked.

After six months of gruelling labour, constant criticism, and unerring devotion to the job that was thrust upon me, I was axed by the Australian Cricket Board with little more than a thank-you. I should be bitter, but I am not. Disappointed yes, because after so many heartbreaks this was a rather ruthless end. I was the fall guy, the player who carried the ACB flag all summer against all the odds. I had to cop it sweet then, and I had to cop my dismissal the same way. Simply, I am a loyalist to the Test cricket scene and an opponent of World Series Cricket. I began the summer determined to lift Australia back to the top of the international cricket ladder, and I felt that the parts were beginning to fall into place late in the summer. The two Tests against Pakistan, a team riddled with World Series Cricketers, proved this as we levelled the series – indeed, we should have won 2–0. So just when the hard yakka was behind us and the future looked rosy, I reluctantly departed the scene as the team's leader.

The news was an enormous setback, initially. I felt that I had shown over the summer that I was learning the trade of captaincy and proving I was a worthy Test batsman. The Board members in their wisdom thought otherwise, and Kim Hughes was given the captaincy for the World Cup with Andrew Hilditch his deputy. My experience apparently counted for something, as I was given the position as third selector on the tour.

What really irked me was that, in effect, we were lambs

to the slaughter anyway. Besides our own cricketing short-comings, we were forced to play on wickets that suited the Englishmen and were alien to us; we copped the bad end of umpiring decisions to a damning degree throughout the Ashes series; and we were crucified by the media in many quarters from beginning to end. All this, combined with the talented opposition which was expected to whitewash us anyway, was just too much.

The hurt that remains is that I tried so hard, and so did the young, raw team that took on so much despite all the odds. My name is now eternally entrenched in the record books as the man who led this country to that ignominious hiding against England and, for the time being anyway, I haven't the chance to redeem myself. As a batsman I intend to make as many runs as possible. Maybe the day will come when once again I will lead this country in the Test arena. Hopefully, a second chance won't be as hard to swallow as the first.

The start to my short reign at the top was rather traumatic, because from the outset in Brisbane both the team and I were subjected to a hammering from the media.

Apparently I was expected, after only one year as captain of Victoria, to walk into the Test team and take control with all the flair and expertise of a Richie Benaud or Ian Chappell. They were apparently the yardstick used by many of the media men, and obviously they took no heed of the fact that I was the third youngest Test captain in Australian history behind William Murdock, 25, and Ian Craig, 22, and that I was in charge of a raw team in Test ranks. When I won the toss and decided to bat in Brisbane – as any captain would have and as Mike Brearley declared he would – and Australia crashed to 6–26, I was immediately branded a fool. Everybody was wise after the event, but all I copped was criticism. I expected the English press to seize on me and immediately call for my head – which they did – because that is apparently part of the off-field battle in a psychological warfare. They pouted at once that I couldn't handle the situation and had to be replaced. What nonsense some of them write. They gave me just enough time to flip a coin before they launched into me, boots and all.

What upset me more was that sections of the Australian media – especially those headhunters from Sydney – were unthinking enough to jump on the bandwagon and run down the team and myself from that minute on. The personal criticism was hard enough to swallow, but the general treatment of the team was often shoddy. There were stories during the summer that simply were not constructive. At one stage, a couple of Sydney newspapers called for mass sackings, but offered no alternative players.

The whole team suffered and, instead of gaining support from the media, we were put under increasing pressure. For instance, whenever we did poorly we were roasted for 'just another expected flop', without credit being given to the tourists' fine bowling on wickets that suited them. Then, when Australia did well, it was a case of England blowing the ball-game, with Australia's fine work glossed over with minute credit. All this had a demoralizing effect on the team. With constant calls for axings there was always an uneasiness among the players.

We expect this sort of treatment when in England or elsewhere overseas, but we felt we deserved a better deal from many of the media people. Basically, the Melbourne media was the only section of the touring press party that showed any faith in us. We were crucified in Sydney, from go to whoa, and I make no bones about it.

While we were always under pressure, the media indirectly helped England by giving them a golden run, rarely twisting the knife when it deserved to be. I will go as far as using an example between Mike Brearley and myself. I was forever on the rack for my leadership (and given scant credit for scoring two centuries and topping the aggregates for Australia), while Brearley escaped criticism with extraordinary luck throughout the summer. He emerged almost untainted, after struggling for a paltry 37 runs in his initial six Test innings, when an Australian would have been burnt at the stake for such a pathetic showing. Yet nobody seriously queried his place in the team, because he was captain and England led 2–1 at that stage. The stock answer was something like, 'Oh, but he is such a good captain that his batting doesn't matter all that much'. No such courtesies were extended to me, or any of my team-mates.

9

Mike Brearley would not have survived too long under the Australian system. But his team carried him, and he accepted the accolades for the Ashes triumph, without a ripple of complaint about his inability to contribute to the team's total – which is what a batsman is in the side to do. Maybe nice guys do win after all.

While on the subject of captaincy, I would like to discuss the difference between the Australian and English systems of selecting a captain. Australia selects a team and then picks a skipper, while England nominates a captain who then helps choose the rest of the players in the team. The Englishmen are claiming a victory for their system after this campaign, but I don't agree. I believe a captain should lead by example on the field and, in my opinion, Brearley fell far short in that department.

Mike Brearley, who is writing *The Ashes Retained* about this series, passed these comments on the different systems. I find them enlightening:

England usually appoints a captain for a series and from then on the captain is involved in the selection of the side. Personally I think that is the right approach. Ideally the captain is also going to be well worth his place in the team because it is much easier to gain respect from the other players, especially initially, if they respect you as a player. That makes it easier to tell another player that he is not playing right, or that he is not trying hard enough or that his approach is wrong.

So ideally you are going to get the same result whichever way you do it: you get the best eleven players and one of them is an ideal captain. Unfortunately, that doesn't always happen.

That is where I think the English system is better because the captain is totally involved from the start with team selection. The captain is the one who must have confidence in his players – particularly the bowlers – because if he hasn't he is in trouble. If I don't rate someone in the side as a Test bowler it is difficult to hand him the ball with any confidence. And then there is the point of responsibility – the captain gets the blame if the team doesn't perform. So I think that the captain should at

10

least have the chance to forcibly say that he wants a certain player to be included, and what balance he wants the team to take.

I was actually astonished to hear that a captain in Australia is not on the selection committee. I think it is incredible.

Obviously Mike Brearley did not think much of my leadership during the summer, but equally he sympathized with my dilemma. I did not think much of his batting, but then again I envied his position of having exactly the team he wanted throughout the series. We don't see eye-to-eye on a lot of things, but I believe that his thoughts on selection are identical to mine. I think that a captain can have a swifter education if he is involved in the selection panel, where he and the selectors can toss around ideas and sort out a battle-plan with the final line-up.

This could relieve many problems faced by a captain, not the least of which is the difficulty of maintaining harmony in a team. For instance, we endure an unfortunate system whereby a player is not told of his omission from the Test team. This does not help create comradeship and unity in the team. I would prefer to be in a position to talk to the dropped players alone as captain, to explain the decision, after being party to the thinking of the selection committee.

Even if it means contacting a player by telephone from interstate, I think that this would be easier for a player to accept than hearing the news on the radio or from a pressman – or, worse still, from somebody not even connected with the game. Although this would mean more involvement off the field for the captain, it would be a task I would prefer to accept than allow a team-mate to suffer the shock of hearing the news secondhand, without an explanation or a word of encouragement. That may sound strange from a bloke who called for a team manager to help him during the series, so overburdened was I with day-to-day incidentals. But I consider that the first step to victory is a harmonious team, pulling together in the one cause.

I found the pressures of captaincy overpowering during the season, particularly off the field. Although I obviously was not popular with many of the media men, I always tried to keep a rapport with them. Handling the constant flow was at times physically impossible, because I was wanted on-call morning, noon, and night. This was not just for the specialist cricket writers – there were radio talk-back shows; current affairs shows on television; feature writers; magazine writers; and gossip columnists. My private life was virtually non-existent. Eventually, I just had to go for a walk to get peace and quiet and escape the avalanche of telephone calls at home, at the office, and wherever the team stayed.

My wife Helen was marvellous. She put up with a lot, because I cannot remember a day when I put my feet up at home and relaxed. When I wasn't on tour or playing for Australia, Victoria, or my local club Richmond, I was coaching or giving interviews or doing promotions. And, occasionally, I went to work at Graham Yallop Enterprises, although I really did not know where to start once in the office. I prospered because I was Australian captain, but conversely I did not have the time to capitalize on that.

Basically, I am now a professional cricketer. When one considers that the Australian Cricket Board offers about $20,000 for the series against England and Pakistan, and a trip to the World Cup and to India, there is no doubt cricket has moved into the big-time.

Anyway, back to the extraneous matters that kept gnawing away at me during the Ashes campaign. I believe that the wickets for the Tests were not up to standard and, indeed, definitely helped the Englishmen. In Brisbane and Perth the wickets were extraordinarily helpful to the seam bowlers; both wickets in Sydney were paradise strips for the spinners; and even the normally placid Adelaide wicket gave seam bowlers unrealistic help on the opening two days. The pity is that it took a flat Melbourne wicket for Australia to beat England – on the type of wicket we have been reared on, really. Not until Pakistan arrived and played in Melbourne and Perth, and the wickets reverted to a 'normal' state, did our batsmen have a real chance to show their talent. Something has to be done to standardize wickets around Australia and elevate them to first-class standard if our batsmen are to develop to win Tests.

I do not want to dwell on the umpiring decisions, because I have an appreciation of how difficult this job is, especially now with television replays of every appeal. But I fancy that this year Australia came off second-best when questionable decisions were tallied up. Perhaps the umpires were over generous to our English visitors and allowed them many benefits they denied us. Certainly, we were dudded at a few crucial points during the summer when Test matches changed course, and I have recounted several of these times during the book.

The Pakistan section of the summer was turbulent and sensational. Off-field mud-slinging by World Series Cricket contracted players in the Pakistan camp erupted from the outset, and the on-field dramas were so stunning they overshadowed all else. I have plenty to say about the on- and off-field incidents later, but I would point out now that even the propaganda machinery could not camouflage Australia's performances. Australia almost created history in Melbourne in a spirited second innings run-chase, and then whipped the Pakistanis in Perth with style.

I fancy that Australian cricket is now on the way up, and I hope to be there to lead by example. I was a novice captain who learned a great deal during our group initiation in season 1978-9. With men of talent and dedication – and confidence – joining forces I believe we can again return to the top of the international cricket totem pole. The World Cup is a competition greatly divorced from Test cricket, but even there I expect our recent experiences and confidence to hold us in good stead. We already have a series victory against England in the Benson & Hedges Cup series behind us, and our pasting of Pakistan in Perth is another confidence-booster. When we again take on Test matches – against India later this year – I believe we will have served our apprenticeship and be on the threshold of triumphant deeds.

Despite the imbalance of six losses and only two victories during the summer, many bonuses emerged. Australia has a fearsome and penetrating opening-attack in Rodney Hogg and Alan Hurst who, between them, captured an amazing 91 wickets in eight Tests. That rates with the previously-famed combination of Dennis Lillee and Jeff Thomson in

13

the summer of 1974–5 against England – so our striking rate was outstanding. Hogg broke Arthur Mailey's fifty-eight-year-old record for the most number of wickets by an Australian in an Ashes series, with forty-one scalps at an average of 12·85, and he added another 10 wickets to his bag against Pakistan. He gained enormous support from Hurst, who came of age in international cricket with 40 wickets at an average of 22·55 for the summer. This pair repeatedly spreadeagled the opposition's top order batsmen, and will be an integral part of Australia's rise to Test prominence in the near future.

Another bonus was the outstanding leg-spin bowling of Jim Higgs, who captured 19 wickets at 24·63 against England, and who showed he is arguably the best leg-spinner in the world today. Unfortunately, the one-day World Cup competition does not cater for spinners, but Higgs will be one of our key men in India and during future Tests.

On the batting side, Australia unearthed one of the most exciting batsmen seen in the country for years – New South Wales' left-hander Allan Border. He scored 422 runs at the impressive average of 60·29 in five Tests, and went from strength to strength to finish the summer with 276 runs at an everage of 92 against Pakistan. He is a mature player and, at the age of 23, is shaping as a truly outstanding player for this country. Rick Darling, after a disappointing tour of the West Indies and several set-backs during the summer came of age and finished with 375 runs at 37·50 in five Tests. I believe he is one of the most talented players in the country at the age of 21, and has the potential to become a champion opening-batsman. Kim Hughes also played several fine innings, and he established himself with 457 runs at an average of 30·46 in eight Tests. When wicketkeeper Kevin Wright is included, one can see that Australia has the nucleus of a top side. In only four Tests, Wright held twenty-one catches and executed a stumping. His work is safe and polished, often brilliant. He should be around for many years to come.

The World Cup will be important to Australia because the world will be gauging our progress after this domestic season. The touring party to carry Australia's flag is:

Allan Border (New South Wales), 23
Gary Cosier (Queensland), 25
Rick Darling (South Australia), 21
Geoff Dymock (Queensland), 33
Andrew Hilditch (New South Wales), 21
Rodney Hogg (South Australia), 28
Kim Hughes (Western Australia), 25
Alan Hurst (Victoria), 28
Trevor Laughlin (Victoria), 28
Jeff Moss (Victoria), 31
Graeme Porter (Western Australia), 24
Dav Whatmore (Victoria), 25
Kevin Wright (Western Australia), 26
and myself.

Victorian Cricket Association secretary David Richards was appointed manager/treasurer of the tour, and we look forward to a tour that would prove a stepping stone to this country's sporting fortunes.

That is the future, but now I would like to reflect on the past. In particular, I would like to quash thought that I had an easy road to the leadership of this country's cricket representation. Then I will look at the summer, blow by painful blow.

2 The Round-up

Born with a silver spoon in his mouth, the critics pouted. Not tough enough to tackle the big-time; he's a Mr Nice Guy and not the type who will handle pressure and lay down the law.

These were some of the disparaging remarks that accompanied my selection as Test skipper, and even followed me as the summer progressed. Unfortunately, some people incorrectly believe that if a bloke goes to a Grammar school he automatically has an easy ride to the top.

I can tell you that just is not on, especially in the competitive world of sport. I fought my way through the ranks like everybody else, depending on practice an enormous amount to try to develop my skills to get the slightest edge on my opponents or competitors. I toured Sri Lanka with the Australian Schoolboys' team in 1971-2 and broke into the Victorian team, after several seasons with Richmond, the following summer. Six innings netted me 173 runs at 28·33. To gain further experience I headed to England, like so many young cricketers, for a tilt with Walsall in the Birmingham League. I didn't make the Victorian team the following season but returned to score 472 runs at an average of 31·46 in 1974-5. That summer included a score of 100 not out against South Australia at the Melbourne Cricket Ground, and was the start of serious steps forward.

As is my custom, I began the season slowly in the eventful summer of 1975-6, with only 31 runs in the opening three Shield matches. Then I hit a purple patch, with scores of 79 and 62 against Ian Chappell's South Australians and 108 not out and 95 against New South Wales. These few performances, to my surprise, resulted in Test selection.

I replaced Rick McCosker, who had not been having a good series against the West Indies, in the Fourth Test team for Sydney. The dropping of McCosker angered Ian Chappell and his team-mates, and I copped the brunt of their annoyance.

16

I may have been an unassuming guy at the time, but I was rudely awakened to the facts of life at Test level – thanks, or rather no thanks, to Chappell and the rest of the team. I was not exactly welcomed with open arms into the team. In fact, I was lucky to discover my locker in the Australian dressing rooms. To top it off, Chappell figured that if I was selected to replace McCosker, that's exactly what I would do ... at Number 3.

I suppose you could say it was an honour to bat ahead of Ian and Greg Chappell in a Test. But I have no doubts that certain members of that team wanted me to fail and therefore prove that the selectors had erred. Normally, a new batsman could expect to be cradled into the side and be 'hidden' down the order until he gets the feel of the Test atmosphere. There was no such deal for me. I was thrown into the deep end, to sink or swim, and that will live in my memory forever. While I am captain of a team, no batsman will be given the shoddy treatment I received on my Test debut.

So anybody who thinks I was a silver-spoon cricketer can forget it. I managed to pick up 179 runs at an average of 44·75 in three Tests that summer, and I also collected 524 runs for Victoria to top the averages and aggregates with 47·63.

Next summer I again started slowly and I didn't make the Test team. The season was as good as over when I struck form with 134 against Western Australia to lift my season's tally to 372 at an average of 37·20.

Last summer (need I tell you I started slowly?) I was disappointed I didn't catch the selectors' eye until the last Test against India in Adelaide. I was beginning to think I would never make it back, despite the fact that I was captain of Victoria and that my form was red hot at one stage. I scored 105 and 114 not out against New South Wales in Sydney; 35 and 48 against South Australia at the MCG; 79 against New South Wales at the MCG; and 53 and 30 against Western Australia in Perth before stepping out again for my country.

I couldn't believe the news: not only was I back, I was vice-captain. The vice-captaincy was a 'here today, gone tomorrow' job as, even before the Test started, the Australian Cricket Board announced that Jeff Thomson would help lead the team to the West Indies ahead of me. Still, I made every post a winner in that Adelaide Test and scored my best Test century to date – 121 against the spinning wizards Bedi, Chandra, and Prasanna. The West Indies tour was also successful for me where, despite a broken jaw, I amassed 660 runs at an average of 55.

So even at the start of 1978–9 I counted on nothing. Cricket has been a bumpy road for me; although the pundits were shouting that I was a 'certainty' to captain the Test team, all that really concerned me was to overcome my usual slow start to the cricket season and to make the First Test team. The retirement of Bob Simpson left a giant hole in our side, and the 'retirement' of Jeff Thomson in his bid to join World Series Cricket made the coming Ashes battle doubly difficult.

Simpson returned to the Test arena for the series against India as a caretaker captain at the age of forty-one, and was an outstanding success. He topped the batting averages with 539 runs against India; and, although not as successful in the West Indies with 199 runs at 22·11, his experience was invaluable to all the young players. After serious consideration he called a halt before the start of the home season – news which came hot on the heels of Thomson's decision to join WSC.

Thomson, Australia's gun fast bowler, could not have picked a worse time to pull out of 'national duty'. Besides being vice-captain of the Test team and a player of thirty-two Tests experience, he was one of the most feared fast bowlers in the world, with 145 wickets at 25·52 to prove it. The English must have been laughing even before they left their shores to hear of the turmoil in the Australian team.

Summer 1978–9 then threatened to be one of the most difficult encountered by a Test team, particularly in an Ashes battle. And, as the early days of the summer unfolded, it became more evident that the Test team would lack experience in the highest order. Simpson and Thomson represented ninety-four Tests between them, more than the rest of the touring team to the West Indies combined.

Coupled with the loss of experience was the practical fact that both still had much to offer the national team. Thomson was only just back to his peak after his shoulder injury of 1976–7, and Simpson's wily captaincy, coolness under crisis, and batting skill against spin were important ingredients in the Australian team make-up.

Putting aside that loss (insurmountable as it seemed), Australia readied itself for the opening volleys of the England tour. Unfortunately, there was little to please the selectors in the batting ranks before the First Test, although individual solo efforts did give encouragement: opening batsman Graeme Wood collected a couple of impressive half centuries; Kim Hughes was in top gear with 127 for Western Australia against Queensland; Peter Toohey blazed 158 and 47 against the West for New South Wales; Gary Cosier compiled a 94 for Queensland against Victoria; and, after a lean trot, I came good with 115 against Western Australia while under pressure to ensure my batting spot and possibly the captaincy.

On the bowling scene emerged Rodney Hogg from South Australia. Hogg made immediate headlines when he skittled Geoff Boycott and felled Clive Radley in England's opening encounter of the tour. Alan Hurst was also running hot.

But the negative side was alarming. Opening batsman Rick Darling hadn't shaken off the horrors of the Caribbean tour, Western Australia's Craig Serjeant was in a frightful rut, and David Ogilvie was in a similar predicament. In the bowling department Ian Callen gave only a flutter of his best in the opening game of the season before lack of fitness and form ruled him out of contention; Australia's other speed weapon during the past two series, Western Australia's Wayne Clark, just couldn't get among the wickets at all. As well, wicketkeeper Steve Rixon was not at his peak in the early stages of the summer.

So, as England brushed off its initial defeat by South Australia to build confidence for the First Test in Brisbane, the Test selectors announced the team for the vital first encounter:

G. Yallop (captain), 25, left-hand batsman, 8 Tests
G. Cosier, 25, right-hand batsman, medium-pacer, 16
   Tests
G. Wood, 21, left-hand opening bat, 6 Tests
K. Hughes, 23, right-hand batsman, 3 Tests
P. Toohey, 24, right-hand batsman, 8 Tests
T. Laughlin, 27, left-hand bat, right-arm medium-pacer,
   2 Tests
P. Carlson, 27, right-hand all-rounder, no Tests
J. Maclean, 32, wicketkeeper, no Tests
B. Yardley, 31, right-hand bat, off-spinner, 6 Tests
R. Hogg, 27, right-arm fast bowler, no Tests
A. Hurst, 28, right-arm fast bowler, 2 Tests
J. Higgs, 28, leg-spinner, 4 Tests

There is no question that this team constituted the in-
form players of the summer. However, the basic truth was
that it was a new side under a new captain. The inclusion
of Queenslanders Phil Carlson and John Maclean and
South Australian Rodney Hogg took the number of Test
players employed within twelve months to a staggering
twenty-four. Only regulars Peter Toohey, Gary Cosier,
and paceman Alan Hurst remained from the First Test
team against India a year earlier – and Hurst hadn't played
a Test since that match. The backbone of Australia's
side for the past twelve months had been gutted. Opening
bowlers Thomson and Wayne Clark were gone, as were
Simpson, Craig Serjeant (who was vice-captain for four
Tests against India), wicketkeeper Steve Rixon who had
stood behind the stumps in all of the past ten Tests, and
batsmen Rick Darling and David Ogilvie. So, in effect, I
was at the helm of a brand new combination. The twelve
players totalled only fifty-five Tests between them and
there was no category where experience dominated.
   The five specialist batsmen enjoyed forty-one of those
Tests. of which Cosier contributed sixteen. I was disappointed that he was selected as an opening batsman, as
I felt his experience was wasted in a position that these
days is alien to him. I firmly believe that a team needs two
specialist opening batsmen, particularly in Test cricket and
definitely in an opening match of an Ashes series. Un-

fortunately, the selectors didn't have another opener with imposing enough form to partner Graeme Wood. So Cosier, whose form was good, became the makeshift choice.

The attack was novice in Test ranks with our opening bowlers having only two Tests between them, Trevor Laughlin with the same number, and our spinners Jim Higgs and Bruce Yardley best off with ten between them. However, they did have plenty of first class experience (Hogg excepted), and this was encouraging. The inclusion of wicketkeeper John Maclean added further experience; although he was making his Test debut, after a decade's wait, his astute cricketing brain and years of tough competition made him a valuable choice.

The Englishmen meanwhile went from strength to strength in the First Test build-up. The touring party of sixteen was stacked with experience, youthful potential, and professional skill. Each player in turn enjoyed a taste of success as England won six of the eight lead-up games, losing only to South Australia in its initial first class match and drawing with Victoria in the rain-affected Sir Robert Menzies Memorial Match.

The tourists arrived with 298 Tests between them and a reputation and hunger for success. Recent victories included the whitewash of Pakistan and New Zealand; and their Test team retained the nucleus of the side that beat Australia 3–nil in 1977. The touring party was:

M. Brearley (captain), 36, right-hand batsman, 21 Tests
R. Willis (vice-captain), 29, right-arm fast bowler, 41 Tests
I. Botham, 23, right-hand bat, fast bowler, 11 Tests
G. Boycott, 38, right-hand opening batsman, 74 Tests
P. Edmonds, 27, left-arm spinner, right-hand bat, 13 Tests
J. Emburey, 26, right-arm off-spinner, 1 Test
G. Gooch, 25, right-hand batsman, 7 Tests
D. Gower, 21, left-hand batsman, 6 Tests
M. Hendrick, 30, right-arm fast bowler, 16 Tests
J. Lever, 29, left-arm fast bowler, 13 Tests
G. Miller, 26, right-hand bat, off-spinner, 14 Tests
C. Old, 29, right-arm fast bowler, left-hand bat, 40 Tests
C. Radley, 34, right-hand batsman, 8 Tests

D. Randall, 27, right-hand batsman, 16 Tests

R. Taylor, 37, wicketkeeper, 13 Tests

R. Tolchard, 32, wicketkeeper, right-hand batsman, 4 Tests

I kept close tabs on the England team's progress around the country as they flexed their muscles before the First Test. They unexpectedly lost to South Australia by 32 runs, but that first match was a reasonable exercise to acclimatize in the centre after several useful days in the Adelaide nets. And, although South Australia reached 311 in the first innings (highlighted by 124 by opener John Nash), Bob Willis showed early signs of menacing speed to capture 3 for 61, while spinners Phil Edmonds, with 2 for 53, and Geoff Miller, with 3 for 41, also impressed.

When England batted Geoff Boycott managed 62 before he fell leg before wicket to Rodney Hogg from one of the few deliveries he faced from the fiery speedster. Hogg made quite an impression and fulfilled England's fears that Australia would find a replacement for Thomson. Hogg captured 4 for 43 and put Clive Radley in hospital for an afternoon when a short-pitched delivery hit the right-hander on the forehead. But England still managed 232, and twenty-one-year-old left-hander David Gower showed signs of things to come with a sparkling 73.

Edmonds captured 5 for 52 and Miller 2 for 37 to rout South Australia in the second innings for 149. The disappointing performance from an Australian viewpoint was that of opening batsman Rick Darling. Rick was out hooking for 17 in the first innings after being baited by the England pace attack; and, in the second innings he pulled a delivery once again and was out for 1. Those efforts probably dashed his first Test hopes. Although David Gower completed a fine double with his second innings half century, he gained little support, and England collapsed for 196 to lose the match.

My first encounter with the tourists was at the MCG on November 10 for the inaugural Sir Robert Menzies Memorial Match. Unfortunately, Melbourne's notorious weather wrecked this match as a contest and a result was never on the cards. But I did get a first-hand look at the

22

visitors, although only an hour while in the centre batting before I was bowled by Edmonds for 10. Victoria scored 254 in the rain-affected conditions, and England replied with 8 declared for 241. For England, two innings were significant: Derek Randall looked his fidgety but free-scoring self with 63 as he played with the cocky attitude that won him world acclaim for his 174 in the Centenary Test at the MCG in 1977; and Mike Brearley made a painstaking 116 not out. He is a grafter, basically, and I felt that he didn't handle Alan Hurst well at first, and that Australia might be in for a bit of luck early in England's Test innings. Other than that, the match wasn't of great significance as a build-up to the Test. Victoria managed only 33 without mishap in the second innings before the game ended.

England's team, of course, had not been at full strength on tour until it reached Sydney for the game against New South Wales. It was here that all-rounder Ian Botham played his first game. Botham, one of the hardest hitters of the ball in the game, an unpredictable paceman, and a top competitor and fieldsman, had cut his left hand just before the touring party left England. Although he spent time in the nets bowling and waiting for plaster to be removed, he hadn't ventured into a game. Botham arrived with a big reputation and as a key figure in the balance of the Test team – and his first-up effort against New South Wales demonstrated just why. In England's first innings of 374 he helped himself to a whirlwind 56, and then in New South Wales' second innings he chimed in with 5–51 from 17·2 overs in an exacting workout.

Three other players from the England camp grabbed my attention in this match. Randall followed up his Melbourne form with 110, and there could be no doubt that he relished Australia's fast and bouncy wickets and would be one of our main dangers in the coming series. Off-spinner Geoff Miller warned of his potential when he had New South Wales in a spin with 6–56 in the first innings total of 165. The only aspect of the England team that seemed to give me heart was the failure again of Geoff Boycott. He was caught in the slips from nippy paceman Geoff 'Henry' Lawson in the first innings for 14, and then

23

had to endure rather a torrid time in the five deliveries of the second innings before England clinched a 10-wicket victory. Lawson apparently ignored warnings from umpire Tom Brooks, and gave Boycott five nasty short-pitched deliveries. My spies told me the thirty-eight-year-old Yorkshireman didn't take it very kindly. Maybe pace would be a worry to him, especially the short-pitched delivery during the summer.

The bad news to filter back from that game – beside the fact that England coasted to such a devastating win – was the apparently planned and well-executed demise of Australia's most successful batsman of the past twelve months, Peter Toohey. Toohey loves to drive through the covers off the front foot and the professional Englishmen were fully aware of this. Instead of blocking that shot with a host of fieldsmen in the covers, they invited Toohey to drive with only one fieldsman in that region ... and a bevy of slips and gully men in catching positions. Pete took up the challenge. But, after reaching the 20s in both innings, he fell to that eagerly waiting net of fieldsmen. It was a psychological victory for the tourists. Obviously, they would keep sending Pete invitations throughout the summer as long as he kept on responding.

It was at this time that I was also going through my own drama as I took the Victorian team to Western Australia. Facing up to John Inverarity and his strong team, I had to get runs and handle the team well to earn my place in the Test team and stay in line for the captaincy. I have never been in a winning team in Perth against the West and, although we did remarkably well (I scored 115 and Julien Wiener 100 in the first innings and Jeff Moss 123 not out in the second innings), the game was a draw. My form returned and, as I have already said, we were told of the Test team announcement when we arrived back in Melbourne after the game.

The news came at the same time as the tragic death of my Victorian and Richmond team-mate Paul Melville, who suffered a brain haemorrhage at his Vermont South home.

It was a great shock to us. He was just twenty-one and one of the most popular members of the team both at Richmond and for Victoria. He was omitted from the team

24

to tour Western Australia after a couple of low scores, but he had enormous talent and nobody expected him to be out of the team for long. I think every cricketer who played against him throughout Australia was upset at the news. Certainly, the Victorian and Australian team was shattered and determined to do well for the rest of the season as a tribute to him.

The following week was one of the busiest of my life. I was celebrating my Test captaincy appointment and working out plans to tackle the Englishmen, doing what I could for Paul's family along with all the other saddened friends of the family, and beginning to answer that seemingly endless call by the media. Meanwhile, the Englishmen, having arrived in Brisbane, were red hot for the First Test after a crushing six-wicket victory against Queensland. Bob Willis bowled with ominous speed on a seaming wicket for two wickets, Botham chipped in with three wickets, and Chris Old relished the conditions to collect 4–33. Unfortunately, Queensland decided not to use Gary Cosier as an opening batsman – although he had to take on that role the following week in the Test – and preferred to bat him in his normal position at Number 4. I can appreciate the point that Queensland was looking for new opening batsmen to carry their Sheffield Shield hopes during the rest of the season. But, from a national viewpoint, and especially mine, I was disappointed that the local interest overshadowed the Test requirements. Cosier therefore went into the First Test without having opened an innings during the season.

Queensland managed only 172 after being 1–90, and then England helped itself to 254. Boycott failed again with only 6; Randall once again was in full flight with 66; and Brearley played himself into form with another long innings for 75 not out. Willis upset the applecart in Queensland's second innings when he bowled Cosier for a duck. Indeed, he bowled with fearsome speed again to collect 3–46, and put young opening batsman Max Walters in hospital when he knocked the glass out of the rims of his spectacles. Botham once again proved his value to the team with 5–70 from 20 overs. Australia's only bright spot was a spirited 94 by John Maclean on the eve of the Test – and he missed his century only because he lashed out late in the innings when he was running out of partners. Just as a final warning that the First Test was around the corner and that the Englishmen meant business, Boycott came good with 60, Randall kept his eye in with 47, and Brearley collected another unbeaten score, this time 38.

So, as I headed to Brisbane to gather with the team, the moment of truth had arrived. Little did I know what was in store.

3 The First Killing

Backstabbing within the team had made part of the tour to the West Indies most unpleasant. My first mission when I hit Brisbane was to get the players together, demand that we have total unity within our ranks, and insist that we all pull together for this important Test. I would have preferred the team in Brisbane for as long as a week before the Test just to let them get to know each other. We had, as I have said, a virtually new side, and many of the players really didn't know each other. For instance, I had not played a first-class game with Rodney Hogg, nor did I know if he was a bachelor or what he did for a living or where he lived ... I appreciate that the Queenslanders were competing against England at the time, but that need not have bothered anybody. We could have spied on the tourists, had meetings at evenings when the Queenslanders were free, and also trained together during that period. As it was, we had only a day together to get to know each other – that really was not enough.

At the team meeting on the eve of the Test I think I probably shocked a few of them by saying that I did not want any backstabbing. During the West Indies tour a few unkind words were spoken about a few players behind their backs; and, when it filtered back, naturally there were scenes. I wanted total harmony in this side and warned that I wouldn't tolerate any backstabbing. My message was simple: if you don't have something nice to say about a bloke, say nothing. Or if you do have a legitimate beef, front the man and have it out, don't squeal behind his back and upset the harmony of the side.

The players accepted this and we were off to a flying start. We had a serious discussion on what this match meant to Australia and every cricket follower dissected the tourists, and planned tactics for our initial confrontation. The normal fun and games which followed this analysis showed that we were all in good spirits.

Later, I was chided for my remarks about Australia winning this series 6–0. I copped it sweet, although I was somewhat bewildered about the seriousness with which some people took up that flippant remark from my first press conference at Brisbane airport the previous afternoon. I learned a lesson from that: do not give too much credit to members of the media who obviously know little or nothing about cricket. That now-infamous remark followed what I thought was a ludicrous question about how many Tests Australia would win during the series. Seriously, a ball had not even been bowled, and here I had a chap asking a question like that as I headed to introduce myself to Rodney Hogg. So, in an off-hand way I pronounced a 6–0 victory and, blow me down, I had the headlines – and the criticism – for being cocky, overconfident, and arrogant. As I said, I treated a lot of press questions with a big grain of salt from then on. I realized that, in true police-style tradition, anything you say will be taken down and held against you.

Gary Cosier really provided most of the fun of the team meeting, giving his expert imitation of ABC announcer Norman May. His phantom call of the opening volleys of the team were hysterical. Gary was in good humour, and with good reason, for he had just signed a ten-year contract reportedly worth about $500,000 to remain in Brisbane to play cricket and open a company to deal in promotions.

As he put it, 'I won't have to worry about money for the rest of my life'. That theme was beginning to run through the team as the Australian Cricket Board's generous payments along with money from sponsors made the cricketers' lot very comfortable.

England named its First Test team and I did not think there were any surprises. The players either had form or were specialists in batting positions – apart from Graham Gooch who was, in my opinion, lacking in both departments. The team then was: Mike Brearley (captain), Bob Willis (vice-captain), Geoff Boycott, Graham Gooch, Derek Randall, David Gower, Ian Botham, Geoff Miller, Bob Taylor, Phil Edmonds, Chris Old, and John Lever as twelfth man. Australia left out all-rounder Phil Carlson, which did not meet with local approval, naturally enough. But that was the only way we could have a reasonably balanced side, particularly as we had Cosier who could lend a hand with his slow-medium deliveries to complement his batting.

All the goodwill one expects before the actual battle begins on the field was shot to ribbons outside the dressing-rooms before the start of play on the opening day. Mike Brearley, who I found a likeable-enough bloke, walked up to me and said, almost off-hand, 'The boys don't want to have a drink with you at the end of each day's play'. I was dumbfounded, but simply said that, if that was what he wanted, we would not be drinking with them then. The players were annoyed when I told them, and their reaction was that the Poms could 'go jump'. From then on, there was always an uneasy feeling about having a drink with the English players. That should never have been the case.

I thought that was rotten, because I believe that when in Rome you should do as the Romans do. As it turned out only three players came regularly for a drink – Ian Botham, David Gower, and Chris Old – and their companionship was always welcome. More's the pity that a chat about the day's play or anything in general was not a regular feature of the summer as it usually is. It would have been especially beneficial to the younger players. Generally, the Englishmen were in and out of their dressing-rooms as quickly as possible, and no doubt back at the hotel while we were just opening the tops of a few bottles to relax. They have their way of doing things and we have ours, but I would have been happier had they bent a little occasionally and, win or lose on a given day, done the right thing by Australian standards and spent a few lousy minutes having a friendly chat and a drink with the Australian team.

Fortunately, I didn't have time to brood over Brearley's request because I was soon in the centre inspecting the wicket and waiting for the official pre-match ceremonies. I talked to the selectors about the wicket, which I thought would be a good batting wicket, and they agreed. Then three skydiving parachutists, trailed by flags of England, Australia, and Queensland descended on to the Gabba with a specially minted medallion to commemorate the fiftieth anniversary of Tests in Queensland. After both sides were introduced to the State Governor, Sir James Ramsay, the crunch came.

I was aware that Mike Brearley would bat if he won the toss; so, naturally, would I in this First Test of the Ashes campaign. The wicket looked anything but venomous: there was a bit of patchy grass but nothing more; and after a few early troubles which are normally associated with a first day wicket, nobody expected too many hassles.

How wrong could you be? I won the toss and how I wish now that I hadn't. There were, however, no second thoughts whatsoever about batting. And so, after months of build-up, and years of waiting for this moment when I would captain Australia, England took the field as Graeme Wood and Gary Cosier took block.

What a disaster. Wood, who is accustomed to running sharp singles with Ric Charlesworth in Perth, took a single from the first delivery from Bob Willis. And, as if it were contagious, Gary Cosier – far from the swiftest runner in the business – repeated the dose. The English fieldsmen were alerted to them immediately and, when Wood called for another single from the fifth ball of the Test, Cosier just kept running back to the pavilion. Wood had pushed the delivery into the covers and headed off; but David Gower, the fleetest fieldsman in the side, swooped on the ball and his underarm shy at the stumps caught Cosier with his bat in the air and out of his ground. That injudicious single left Australia 1–2. Clearly we could not afford to hand over wickets like that. I think that Cosier's run out was evidence enough that a Test team requires two specialist opening batsmen. Not just for the obvious reasons of handling the new ball, but because they are alert to taking sharp singles to break up a field. Cosier is more the type of player who breaks up an attack later in the order by clouting a few deliveries out of sight, not by trying to dash down the wicket three times in five balls.

Peter Toohey lasted just nine minutes to score one. He was the first to appreciate just how much movement the wicket was providing the seam attack of Willis and Chris Old, who relish such conditions He played and missed three times, and never looked like getting on top Finally, he attempted a rather airy and ambitious on-drive to a

30

Willis delivery that pitched about off-stump, and was bowled between rather a large gap between bat and pad. Australia was 2-5, and in I walked wondering what the hell had happened to that good batting wicket I thought I saw only twelve minutes earlier.

I couldn't believe it. Old was swinging the ball wildly and then making it seam sharply off the wicket – all this, and he was deadly accurate too, so he made you play every ball. Willis was also fast and seaming the ball. So life in the centre was anything but comfortable. All I wanted to do was stick around, hoping that this unbelievable early life would die out after lunch. Wood and I played and missed to an agonizing point, but we survived somehow. You could not do any more than play straight on this wicket, because the ball deviated so much that even playing the correct line you often missed the ball by a considerable margin. It was, however, just a matter of time. When Wood was 7, after defying the attack for forty-five minutes, he edged an Old delivery to wicketkeeper Bob Taylor, and we were 3-14. Before the opening hour was thankfully over, we were in the horrors at 3-16. Kim Hughes and I decided to stick as long as possible and hope.

That was easier said than done. The first ball after drinks Old moved a delivery across my body and further off the seam, and I was lucky that Graham Gooch at second slip tried to grab the chance in his over enthusiasm. I was 5 at the time, and the ball appeared to be heading rather cosily to Brearley at first slip. But Gooch made an acrobatic attempt to pluck it in with his right hand and, fortunately for me, he spilled it. Then Kim Hughes had a life, when he was only 1, as an attempted drive off Willis rocketed off the fingers of Old at fourth slip.

But England was not to be denied, and neither Kim nor I was good enough to stop their onslaught. Willis bowled me a brute of a ball – the type that you might see, let alone get, only once a season. It pitched on leg stump and forced me to play at it, but then as if it had hit a minefield it speared across my body and caught the outside edge. It was one of the best deliveries I have ever received, and I didn't have a hope in hell of avoiding the edge. This time Gooch made no mistake and, dejectedly, I left the scene

31

with Australia 4–22. Trevor Laughlin passed me on the way to the wicket, I am sure, in disbelief that as a Number 6 he should be going in with a Test match only seventy-two minutes old.

Worse was to follow, however, as England set about the kill. Botham was given his chance at the bowling crease – I wouldn't be surprised if he threatened to flatten Brearley if he didn't get a piece of this action – and he struck in his opening over. Kim Hughes tried to drive a wide delivery and he edged Bob Taylor another regulation catch. Australia was 5–24, with Hughes out for 4.

The Trevor Laughlin exited for 2 as he hooked a Willis bouncer with radar accuracy to substitute John Lever at fine leg. We were 6–26 after only fourteen overs, and no recognized batsman had reached double figures. I was in a state of shock to put it mildly. I thought, 'What in the world have we got here?', even though at that stage I was unaware that the statisticians were ogling the record books and readying themselves to nail us as the team to score the least number of runs in a Test innings for Australia – 36 at Birmingham in 1902 being the previous 'record'. Someone had to take the long handle or the England pacemen had to break down and follow Chris Old off the field where he was repairing an injured finger. Or maybe somebody would pinch me and I would wake up from a terrible nightmare.

Thankfully, local hero John Maclean and hard-hitting Bruce Yardley staged a minor revival with a 27-run partnership (actually, since they doubled the score of the top six batsmen, I suppose you could say it was a big revival). They played sensibly, hitting the loose deliveries, and defending the best they could to the rest. Yardley chanced his arm once too often, however, and was caught at the wicket from Willis' bowling after helping himself to two boundaries in his half-hour stay. Maclean's and Yardley's uninhibited hitting must have rubbed off on Rodney Hogg, because he went in and immediately lashed out with a mixture of fine cuts and powerful drives and a few less copybook shots that were all effective. The wicket had lost much of its early life but was still not easy to bat on. Interestingly, the Englishmen were showing signs of frustration as our total passed 100 – a very pleasant sight indeed.

The pair added 60 runs in seventy-nine minutes to carry us to 8–113, but that was as far as we went really. Botham, who had Hogg caught at the wicket, presented Bob Taylor with his fifth catch of the innings when he removed Alan Hurst for a duck, and then Chris Old celebrated his return to the field to wrap up the innings when he bowled Jim Higgs for 1 to give him 2–24 in a menacing display. Maclean was unconquered on 33 after a sterling effort of defying the attack for two and a quarter hours; justly, he received a standing ovation from his home crowd to help him remember his Test debut.

Australia's total was far from impressive at 116, but by the same token it was almost more than anybody could have hoped for after it had been 6–26. We had simply been trapped on a dangerous wicket that had hidden itself for several days. Even the curator Jack McAndrew was stunned. He had not put the covers on overnight to allow the strip to breathe, and freely advised all and sundry before play that he would bat and that there would be plenty of runs in the pitch. Well, if 116 was to be plenty of runs, I felt we had a reasonable chance of ripping into the England batsmen in the same way that Willis, Botham, and Old had mauled us. Willis took the bowling honours with 4–44 from fourteen overs, and his height and pace caused insurmountable problems to all batsmen Botham chimed in with 3–40 and Old 2–24. Spinner Phil Elmonds bowled only one maiden over, so that is how obvious it was that seam bowling was the order of the day. There was not much I could really say to the fellows before we went into the field except that whatever the wicket offered we had to exploit it to get ourselves back into the game and restore our honour.

Our first success came after only twenty minutes and 2 runs when Rodney Hogg made a delivery drag in sharply from outside Graham Gooch's off stump and his 'cover-up' of bat, glove, and body sent the ball ballooning to Trevor Laughlin at gully. That was just what the doctor ordered: not only did we have a breakthrough early, but the Englishmen began to look anxiously at the wicket and worry about the tricks it still might have even late in the day. However, despite many close calls by Geoff Boycott and Derek Randall, we just could not get a run-on. Hogg surprised me after his early breakthrough by handing me the ball and calling for a rest. That was the first time I have ever been asked to relieve a bowler when he had 1–1 in his first Test or in any game for that matter. But it was to become a regular occurrence during the season, and I have saved my thoughts on the matter for a later stage of this book.

Hogg returned later in the day and with him came the break we sorely needed – the scalp of bogey man Geoff Boycott. Boycott edged a lifting delivery to Kim Hughes at third slip and left the scene only 13 runs to his credit in a total of 38 in an hour and a half's batting time. I wasn't so concerned that Boycott might carve us up, but rather that he would just stick about long enough to make it easy for the rest of the batsmen. This man Hogg had 2–2, and he had shown a speed and accuracy that promised much as the series progressed. He certainly had a psychological edge over Boycott, having dismissed him three times in their only three encounters.

England sent Bob Taylor in to join Randall as a night-watchman and they deprived us of further success while taking the total to 2–60 at stumps. I was not very pleased about play being called off fifteen minutes before the scheduled time, as obviously Randall talked the umpires into it after a couple of failed attempts. The weather was overcast but wasn't as bad when we left the field as it was earlier. I desperately wanted Taylor out and a crack, no matter how short, at the next batsman before stumps. The decision to quit early just about summed up our day.

I couldn't wait to get to the Gabba the next morning, a humid Saturday, hoping to find as much life in the pitch as the Englishmen found the previous day. So I pinned my faith in the pace of Hogg and Hurst with support from Laughlin and Cosier. That my judgement wasn't re-warded was basically my own fault. Randall, who resumed at 43, went on to reach his half-century with eight 4s and a 6 in just under two hours; and that was when we had a golden opportunity to break through. At 52, he edged a rearing delivery from Hogg, and the ball diverted to me at first slip. I should have swallowed it, but it hit me in the midriff and I juggled it three times as I fell backwards before it rolled over my shoulder. I was distraught, but the damage was done. And so, after our bowlers toiled luck-lessly, Randall and Taylor survived until lunch, although they added only 30 runs. Randall was not his usual aggres-sive self, but he was quick to capitalize on any deliveries which he could hook or cover drive. Taylor was just as big a headache as Randall's foil. He played a straight bat to everything and forced our bowlers to expend enormous time and effort without success. Fortunately the drought broke when Randall ran out of patience and tried to ham-mer a delivery through covers from Hurst. His thick out-side edge travelled like a rocket past gully and everybody – Randall, myself, and all the fieldsmen – were amazed when Trevor Laughlin threw out his right hand to take an exceptional catch. Finally, after 220 minutes in which he had frayed us for ten 4s and a 6, Randall was out of the way. England was 3–111 (Lord Nelson had done the trick again!) and Laughlin's catch inspired the team with a new lease of life and the spirit to fight back.

Just 9 runs later as England squeezed to a lead, Hogg accounted for Mike Brearley. The England skipper con-tributed only 6 runs before he tried to turn a leg-side delivery and edged John Maclean a low catch which he took well. Then, suddenly, England were 5–120, just 4 runs ahead when Hurst ended Taylor's marathon defiance of 170 minutes by trapping him in front of his stumps for 20. Three wickets had fallen for only 9 runs and we were running hot and in the mood to climb right back into contention.

But I suppose fortune favours the brave, and Ian Botham certainly had his share of luck as he took the long handle to our bowlers with telling results. He slashed a Hurst delivery through gully's hands; miscued a couple of hooks which fell safely; at 26 he edged a Laughlin delivery that didn't quite carry to Maclean; and then he sent an on-drive just out of Higgs' reach from Yardley's off-spin.

With David Gower combining a mixture of elegant cuts and drives with repeated slashes outside the off-stump the pair suddenly had a 50-run partnership on the board in only sixty-one minutes and by then England had skipped away to 5–176. We were back to the grindstone as the 200 came and went. And, by the time the second new ball was due – I had to take it immediately to break this stand – Hogg and Hurst were looking for a shady tree and cool drink. But they bounced back and broke the 95-run union, with Hogg finding Botham's top-edge when hooking, and Hurst finally touching that elusive Gower edge after so many frustrating misses.

Botham's innings of 49 was invaluable to England, and he thwarted us with his daredevil tactics that came off at every risky attempt. He also played a few thundering drives and pulls. Basically, he was the most difficult man to bowl at and set a field to in the innings. He went to the wicket with England in somewhat of a slump at 5–120, and when he left he had seen them safely to 6–215, and a lead of 99. Gower went just four runs later for 44, as so often happens when a big partnership is broken. Hogg pressed home the new-ball advantage with the scalp of Phil Edmonds for 1 with the score then at 8–226. Edmonds edged a leg-glance and Maclean dived full length to the left to snare a spectacular grab. He could not possibly have travelled another centimetre, and he could not have wanted a finer catch on his debut.

After those three wickets in 11 runs I hoped to wrap up the innings quickly but, unfortunately, Hogg and Hurst had run their race. The pressure could not be maintained on Geoff Miller and Chris Old, two rather useful batsmen to have coming in at Number 8 and Number 10, as it was with Taylor previously acting out his role as a nightwatchman. So we had to settle with 8–257 by stumps and a deficit of 141. England scored only 197 runs during the day, which was curtailed by thirty-five minutes because of noon rain and poor light five minutes before stumps – so at least they had not run all over us. The frustration was beginning to tell, however. Every time we played at a delivery we were out; yet their batsmen played and missed so often that it was beginning to gnaw at all of us after a while. I suppose we all wanted so desperately to do well that, when success didn't come, we were not experienced enough in Test cricket to take it in our stride and wait for it. That's where the Englishmen taught us so much in their innings. They played and missed again and again, but didn't get flustered, and just waited until the pieces fell back into place.

We had to wait for more than an hour on the third day to finish the England first innings at 286. Miller's hour and a half innings ended at 27 when he played back to a Hogg delivery, and then Bob Willis presented John Maclean with his fifth catch of the innings to complete a fine debut for the Queenslander. Old was unbeaten on 29, and his contribution to the England team with both bat and ball was damaging. Hogg returned the fine figures of 6–74 from 28 overs and Hurst 4–93 from 27·4 overs to share all the honours. How I would have liked to have seen them in action first on this wicket.

Under the circumstances, I was happy enough to restrict England's lead to 170. But, with more than half the Test remaining, I drummed into the players the need to bat sensibly to get us out of trouble. So our batting reputation was on the line again as Wood and Cosier left the pavilion, this time Cosier taking block to Willis.

Crash. Cosier played forward to Willis' first delivery of the innings, left a gap between bat and pad, and his stumps went flying. What a disastrous start: 1–0 and Cosier back in the pavilion once again. An opening batsman he was not, and there was no way we could persevere with him in that position for the good of the side and for his own good. He could hardly believe it, but there it was. He had just 1 run to his credit in two innings in the Test as an opening batsman. Peter Toohey, trying not to let himself fall into the 'gap between bat and pad' error that cost him his wicket in the first innings, hardly had a look-in. He survived an appeal for l.b.w. by Ian Botham who was bowling into the breeze with the new ball, but there was no escaping the next appeal in the same over. Toohey was out for 1; and Australia, after just eight minutes, was 2–2.

I made that disconcerting path across the Gabba dog track on to the field to yet again face the music. 'Not again', I thought to myself as I went to the crease. 'I was here at 2–5 in the first innings and we were soon 6–26, and here I am again at 2–2. Don't tell me it's going to happen all over

again. It just couldn't. If I don't stay in it will be a schemoz-
zel and we will be laughed at from here to Kingdom Come.'
I don't mind telling you I felt the pressure on me more than
ever in my life as I took block, and I was as toey as a two-
year-old colt.

Graeme Wood and I survived to lunch and took the score
to 20. After the interval we played fairly well to carry the
total to 49, before Old trapped Wood in front of his stumps
for 19. Graeme's wicket was a blow, because he was starting
to slip into gear and make the bowlers really work hard
just to contain him. So were were 3–49 and still 121 runs
in arrears when Kim Hughes joined me. He immediately
hopped into any loose deliveries and, as I started to unleash
a few shots myself, we found that runs were not that hard
to come by. My cut was working well, while Kim clubbed
a 6 over square leg from Willis to show that there was still
fight and a touch of aggression in this side yet. When the
loose deliveries came he clobbered them, but otherwise we
contented ourselves with dogged defence and an occasional
single to keep the fieldsmen on their toes. As we progressed
with our rearguard action the Englishmen became a little
uptight; and as we started to put the pressure on them a few
of them lost their cool. By tea the score eased to 3–102 as I
reached my half-century after 132 minutes – a satisfying
feeling, although I knew the job was nowhere near started,
really.

After the interval Kim and I employed the same tactics:
defend everything on the stumps, nudge singles wherever
we could and give the loose ball everything it deserved. We
were content to see out 12 overs from Geoff Miller for only
14 runs, and I think that also began to annoy the Englishmen, who obviously thought that both Kim and I were certain to crack and play a rash shot.

Our century partnership took 165 minutes, and the pressure was right on. Kim reached his half-century after three
hours, and by stumps we were still together when poor light
stopped play twenty-five minutes early. We had taken the
score to 3–157, just thirteen runs short of making England
bat again, and that was a great relief. As I headed home
that night to the hotel, more than ready for the rest day to

38

relax my weary bones and throbbing brain, I had a self-satisfaction in our progress that day. We had shown that we could fight back and that the England bowlers could be countered, and that fight justified my belief in the individual talents of the players in the side. Our bowlers had toiled well without much luck, and after another bitterly disappointing start, our batsmen were showing their worth.

Rain, torrential as apparently only Brisbane can bucket it down, ruined a planned fishing trip to the Queensland coast on the rest day, but that didn't really bother me very much. Kim and I and the rest of the batsmen had to bat through the following day to ensure a safe position, and that was all that mattered. When we resumed, Kim and I set ourselves an immediate target of seeing out the second new ball, which was only 13 overs away. Actually, we found runs easier than at any stage in the opening hour, when we added 40 runs to coast past our 150-run union in 236 minutes.

I posted my century when I pushed a single to mid-on during the second new ball assault. I was delighted, naturally enough, but I realized I had to put my head down again and stick around to push Australia to safety. I didn't know until later that I was the first Australian captain to score a century in his first Test as leader against England. That information was a thrill, especially as when I went to the wicket I could think of nothing but survival – a century was the furthest thing from my mind.

Kim and I had just about completed our aim when Willis, who was suffering with blistered feet, got me out during his last over with the new ball. Willis sent down a half-volley, and I thought to myself, 'more honey for the bear', and stepped into it to drive. The ball went back like a rocket low to his right, and he just threw out his hand and plucked in a most casual catch. It was a magic catch and I couldn't believe it.

I felt like I had made a duck instead of a century as I left the field, so disappointed was I that I had gone out when Australia needed me to score more runs. But I did have 102 to my credit and I thought that, now I had shown the way with almost six hours at the wicket, the other blokes might follow suit. Kim and I put on 170 (the first innings deficit we faced) but we were only 49 runs ahead when I departed, and we needed some good scoring and occupation of the crease for long periods by the other batsmen.

That is exactly what didn't happen. Trevor Laughlin lasted only thirteen minutes for 5 runs before he was out l.b.w. to Chris Old. At virtually 5–58 we were back in hot water. John Maclean lingered on for an hour for 15 runs before he was also adjudged l.b.w. trying to sweep Miller. But at least the score had advanced to 6–261 by then. Bruce Yardley helped Hughes through to tea and carried the score to 303 and a lead of 133, and there was still every chance that we could see out the day and make an England victory most difficult. We were foiled again, however, as Miller drifted a delivery past Yardley's fending bat and Brearley held the catch to remove our hard-hitting right-hander for 16 after almost an hour and a quarter.

Hogg enjoyed a 29-run stand with Hughes in forty-two minutes before his leg-stump was rattled by an inswinger from Ian Botham at 16; and then, next ball, Botham uprooted Hurst's off-stump with a full toss.

Kim, with no option now but to lash out, hoisted a catch to Phil Edmonds at mid-wicket from a Willis delivery, and that ended our innings at 339. Overall that was a reasonable tally considering the start of 2-2 under the strain of a 170-run deficit. At least it showed we were capable of scoring runs. But it left us only 169 runs in front with forty-five minutes and a full fifth day to play. Unless rain interfered we stood only a faint hope of surviving this first encounter.

Kim Hughes' innings of 127 in 476 minutes of dedicated and intelligent batting was a gem. I doubt we will see another innings like that one. It was so uncharacteristic as he knuckled down to the task at hand, resisted tempting half-volleys in the crisis but hammered them when the pressure was eased, and never wavered from the challenge. He timed the ball magnificently. When I was with him I reached my century first but at no stage was I hitting the ball as crisply. He destroyed the England attack with a combination of faultless resistance and then devastating aggression, pacing himself as the situation demanded. Normally Kim tries to set his own pace and stick to it. But in this innings he allowed the circumstances to determine how he would bat and he did it beautifully. It was one of the classic innings of the series.

We were again desperately unlucky not to have had two of the Englishmen out before stumps. Boycott survived an l.b.w. decision from a Hogg delivery when he played back on to his stumps in the second over of the innings, and Gooch was perilously close to a similar fate from a Hurst delivery. But they survived and, at 0–16, required only 154 during the last day's play.

Against all the odds we forced England to scrounge for every run in the opening session as we captured 3-66. Gooch fell to Hogg's first ball in the second over of the day when he edged a low and fast chance to Bruce Yardley at third slip. He contributed only 2 and England were 1–16, not having added to the overnight score. Then Peter Toohey threw out Geoff Boycott for 16 with a direct hit at the striker's end from covers, and the score was 2–37. Randall, the man who spaced us in the first innings and who had enjoyed a run feast of more than 200 runs on the Gabba wicket during the past week, went for his shots once again and quickly took the score to 50. He was lucky to survive an l.b.w. appeal from Hurst when he was 17 but, other than that, he didn't give us a look-in. We maintained the pressure, however, when Brearley bottom-edged a cut shot to Yardley and was caught at the wicket for 13 to keep us in with a chance as England slipped to 3–74.

By lunch England was 3–82, and Randall and David Gower took only 109 minutes to wipe off the 88 runs needed to end the Test at 3.15 p.m. Randall's 74 not out, to follow his first innings 75, was the key, while Gower collected a pair of 40s in another valuable contribution to the victory with 48 not out to go with his earlier 44. England's win in Brisbane was its first for forty-two years and the 7-wicket margin was conclusive enough.

Losers cannot expect praise but, considering our effort in forcing the game to the final afternoon after our dreadful start. I felt we had shown enough to be given the benefit of any doubts about our potential. No way. I copped both barrels for not bowling Jim Higgs earlier and, more specifically, for not giving him a bevy of fieldsmen around the bat as soon as he took the ball.

What annoyed me was that most of the critics had not seen Higgs even bowl before, let alone know his traits. Jim and I have played together for a number of years, particularly for Richmond and Victoria, and we have worked out to a tee what field placings suit him best when he begins to bowl. He takes a while to adjust to his line and length and wants a couple of overs with the field in 'normal' positions. His style of bowling is complex, and he likes to work on a batsman for an over or so before he thinks about bringing in a few close-in fieldsmen. He is prone to bowl a few loose deliveries and he wants them cut off to keep a batsman at his end to work him out. If you put men up immediately he gets jittery and tends to waver in line and length. That's the way he is and that's the way we operate. It's all well and good people saying I should have had half the team sitting around the batsmen to put them under pressure, but what pressure would there have been if Higgs couldn't bowl well and was carted all around the ground?

That was just one of the criticisms that overrode the fightback of the team and that was a general disappointment. We had gone into the Test as rank outsiders and we forced England into the final day with only two and a bit hours to play. Considering our dilemmas during the match I felt we did reasonably well. Perhaps it was because we did so well in the middle stages and raised hopes of saving or even winning the match that we sparked such final bitter disappointment. Regardless, we had to suffer the abuse in silence, even though we felt personally disappointed with the result. Disappointed but not down-hearted, I must add. There was much to encourage us from the Test, obvious holes to fill, and a ray of sunshine for the games ahead.

4 Fleeced

Before I left the Gabba I wandered to the secretary's office to see Bill McCarthy about a few minor details and he told me the Second Test team had been announced: Jim Higgs and Trevor Laughlin were out, and Geoff Dymock and Rick Darling were in. The selectors had gone and so I felt it was up to me to tell Higgs and Laughlin about the team before the press descended on them or they discovered the news from a taxi driver. I went back to the dressing-rooms and called for Trevor Laughlin to come outside. He didn't come, so I went inside. 'I know what you're about to say. I guessed it', Trevor said. Then I called Jim Higgs outside and told him, as he said in his normal jovial way, 'What's the problem, skip.' He just accepted it in his normal un-emotional way and said, 'Fair enough', and we went back into the rooms for a drink.

That was not a very pleasant moment. Besides being part of my team for Australia and Victoria (and Richmond for Higgs), they are mates of mine and blokes with whom I had toured the West Indies. Both players accepted the fact that they had to go back to Sheffield Shield cricket and perform well to force their way back into the Test team. But I still think that sort of selection method is not a good system. The team was chosen during the afternoon and announced to all-and-sundry just after the end of the game. I think in such circumstances the chairman of selectors could come into the rooms and explain to the person or players involved why they have been omitted. It would put the players at ease a little, knowing what they have to do to get back, where they went wrong, and any other question that may arise. I remember when I wasn't selected in the Test team in 1976-7 after playing the previous summer that I was dejected. Any player is naturally disappointed, and I half expected it.

That unpleasant task completed, Trevor, Jim and I headed to Sydney for the Shield match against New South Wales. I scored a century in the first innings and 48 in the second. My form was tops at that stage, having three centuries in three matches to my name. I was hitting the ball well and looking forward to Perth ... where I had started my run with that 115 against Western Australia.

Then came the bad news. Word kept coming back that Western Australia routed England, then that England routed Western Australia, and then that the whole process was repeated and that England had won the game in two days by 140 runs. 'What the hell is going on over there', I thought. Just three weeks earlier Western Australia and Victoria scored more than 1000 runs without a hitch on a magnificent batting wicket, and now we had scores of 144 and 126 to England and 52 and 78 to Western Australia. I studied that scorecard closely because Western Australia had not been beaten for almost three years and normally gives the touring side a hiding. Firstly, England batted and crashed to 6–31 before reserve wicketkeeper Roger Tolchard came to the rescue with an unbeaten 61. Then not a single West Australian could reach double figures in a total of 52, as Mike Hendrick captured 5–11 off only 5·4 overs, and Botham got 4–16 from 9 overs. The whole débâcle lasted only 137 minutes. England found five batsmen to reach double figures in its second innings for 126, and then Western Australia crumbled again. In 116 minutes the Western Australian team could manage only 46 runs for the loss of six wickets by stumps on the second day and, with a breezy 38 not out by Bruce Yardley, mustered 78 at the end.

There was obviously something drastically different between that wicket and the one used for the Shield match a few weeks earlier, and the unravelling of that mystery was to be my first job once I hit the West.

The wicket simply had to wait once I hit Perth. News was out that West Australian opening batsman Graeme Wood had signed only a one-year contract with the Australian Cricket Board. All other players had signed a two-year contract which the Board put forward and some of them signed it against their better judgement, as they wanted only a one-year contract.

So there was an uneasy situation. A few players were upset, and a number of them wanted to find out why Wood was allowed to sign for one year when they were told they had no option but to sign for two. As they were so anxious about the matter, I rang the ACB chairman Mr Bob Parish in Melbourne and tried to sort out the matter. He told me that Wood's was a special case but that this would not happen again. I passed on the information I had to the players and we had to accept it, although feelings were still running a little high in some quarters.

I don't think people were particularly upset with Graeme Wood. They were concerned that they had not been given the same chance. Anyway, I don't think the situation had a great bearing on the team's spirit, and we revved up for the Test.

I then turned my attention to the Perth wicket, asked around for an explanation for the difference between the wicket of three weeks ago and the one for the England game the previous weekend, and came to the conclusion that a fine batting wicket was definitely not on the cards. So, on the morning of the Test after the now familiar skydivers arrived to commemorate Western Australia's 150th anniversary and the introduction to the State Governor Sir Wallace Kyle, I went to the centre for another toss with Mike Brearley. This time I wanted to win the toss, because I had no doubt what was about to happen. The wicket had green ridges on it and it was moist. I was amazed, really, because it was so unlike a Perth track. Why the curator put so much water into it I just do not know. I haven't known a Perth strip to break up badly before so there could not have been too many worries on that side of the argument. Anyway, I fortunately won the toss and I had no hesitation in asking England to bat (and Mike would have had no hesitation about returning the compliment had he called correctly).

The decision was justified within twenty-five minutes as England stumbled to 2–3, thanks to fiery bowling from Rodney Hogg. Graham Gooch, completely out of his depth as an opening batsman, lasted twenty minutes before he finally touched a Hogg delivery and presented John Maclean with a regulation catch. His contribution was 1 and, after his First Test scores of 2 and 2, I could not believe our fortune that England persevered with him. Then came the jackpot, when Derek Randall injudiciously tried to hook too early in his innings and his top-edge flew to square leg where Wood held the chance with glee. Randall was out for a duck and England's most prolific run-scorer was back in the pavilion. 'Here we go', I thought – a chance to give England what they gave us in the first innings in Brisbane.

Then, with figures of 2–0, Hogg threw me the ball after four overs and said he couldn't bowl another over because he was exhausted. I was flabbergasted, but even pleading for just one more over could not persuade him. He was puffing and gasping, and that was that. Fortunately, with left-armer Geoff Dymock in the side for this Test to share the new ball with Hogg, I had Hurst in reserve. But the pressure was relieved immediately and there was nought I could do about it.

So England survived until lunch at 2–30, with Geoff Boycott treating every delivery like a handgrenade ready to explode, and Mike Brearley playing and missing regularly. But after the break Dymock broke the partnership with Brearley's wicket, an edge to the wicketkeeper from a back-foot slash to a slanted delivery outside the off-stump. Brearley departed for 17 after 116 minutes and, despite the length of time in the centre, he had done little to boost the score and take England from the danger zone. His team was still tottering at 3–41.

We did not strike again all day as Boycott and the free-stroking David Gower played two totally contrasting roles to defy us. Boycott's 360-minute stay for 63 was painstaking although, ideally, what England needed in the circumstances. What annoyed us was that the man simply refused to play shots, even to half-volleys, and at no stage threatened to take the initiative from our bowlers although they were tiring as the day progressed. Actually, I was bored just watching him bat. I think a lot of our players were. The bowlers just kept a good line and he would go back or come forward defensively and prod it back. He did manage to squeeze 31 singles, but they were not even forceful shots – rather, glides or nudges that screwed off the bat. I think Geoff is a nice bloke whose batting leaves a lot to be desired. He has magnificent concentration, but his stroke-making these days is almost non-existent. I think he has almost reached the end of the road.

46

Gower, on the other hand, is the young buck who is on the way up and he showed Boycott exactly what to do. He is a magical player, really, capable of hitting the ball from anywhere, because his eye is so quick to pick up the ball. He took the initiative from the outset, even though England was 3–41, and he reached his 50 in just under two hours. Boycott's half-century took double that time and twice as many scoring shots. Once the ball became older and the bowlers tired as the wicket gave them less encouragement, Gower capitalized on the situation. He cut and drove with awesome power, although he looks so elegant with his timing that he appears to just push the ball into the covers' area.

We took the second new ball forty minutes before stumps to no avail; although Hogg missed Gower from a return catch at 76, and the left-hander was then caught in the gulley from a committed shot to a no-ball at the same score. Then, at 95, he slashed a Hurst delivery through my hands in the gully – although I was lucky to get my fingers to it, as it went like a rocket. Gower had lived dangerously at times, but without the impetus he gave to the scoring, England could still have been in trouble at stumps. He reached his century just five minutes before stumps, after 212 minutes at the crease, and that score included nine boundaries. Boycott did not find the fence once during the day. At stumps England was 3–190. Although we hadn't capitalized on the early life in the wicket to the full extent, we were far from out of the game, because of England's slow scoring rate.

Overnight rain raised hopes that the wicket might again give early assistance, and thankfully this wicket just kept on seaming that day ... and the next ... and ... We desperately needed to break the Boycott-Gower partnership and get into the rest of the England batsmen while the new ball still boasted some shine. Hogg answered our wish, in his second over, with the scalp of Gower for 102. The ball pitched on middle-stump as he bowled round the wicket, and straightened to clip the top of the off-stump. That ended a 158-run partnership in 248 minutes that had wrecked our hopes of a rout.

Hurst then pressed home that early advantage with the

wickets of Ian Botham and Boycott in a three-over burst that cost him only five runs. When Botham reached 11 he was trapped in front of his stumps with the total on 219, and then Hurst repeated the dose to finally end the frustration and stalemate accompanying Boycott's presence with the total on 6–224. Boycott's 77 took a marathon 449 minutes. He was credited with one all-run 4, although he didn't hit the pickets at any stage.

We let ourselves down then by missing Bob Taylor at 0 and 11 from the bowling of Dymock and Hogg, before he holed out to mid-wicket while trying to loft a Yardley off-spin delivery when 12. England's tail continued to wag, however, and the last four wickets after we removed Boycott cost us 65 important runs. Lever contributed 14 before edging a Hurst delivery to Cosier at first slip; the grafting Miller added 40 before Hogg bowled him between bat and pad; and Bob Willis (2) and Mike Hendrick (7 not out) deprived us for another twenty-three minutes.

England's total was eventually an imposing 309 and I could not be satisfied with that after having them 2–3 on a wicket that seamed. They showed us the art of survival, really, and we had to emulate them to get back into the game as we started our innings after tea on the second day. Our bowlers had toiled well without a great deal of luck. Hogg captured 5–65 from 30·5 overs, Hurst 3–70 from 26 overs, and the luckless Dymock 1–72 from 34 overs.

Australia's batting fell apart in that final session and, by stumps, we were in desperate trouble at 4–60. The collapse started when left-arm paceman John Lever trapped Graeme Wood in front of his stumps for 5 with the total only 8. Lever had peppered Wood with a succession of outswingers and then caught him off guard with an inswinger that beat his defensive bat jabbing down too late. Rick Darling, in his comeback innings for Australia, showed plenty of spirit. With the help of Kim Hughes – batting at Number 3 following his Brisbane innings in a dual move to allow out-of-touch Peter Toohey to slip down the order – the score slipped quickly along to 34. But Bob Willis, who hadn't opened with the new ball, came into the attack and sent us reeling. He bowled Kim, played inside the line of a leg-cutter and had his off-stump tilted when he was 16, and I lasted only twenty-three minutes for 3 runs before Willis knocked back my stumps too. The ball pitched about leg and middle and, as I played forward defensively to push it away to the leg side, it cut back sharply off the seam and took my off-stump. As I left the field we were 3–38 but, with Darling in full flight, and Toohey and Cosier to follow as recognized batsmen, I felt we could still climb out of the grave.

Darling and Toohey, two natural stroke-makers, batted almost oblivious to the wicket situation, and took the right approach. They played their normal games and took the runs when they came. So, as the final over of the day began, we were reasonably satisfied at 3–60. Then came the inexplicable run-out of Rick for 25. Peter Toohey played the second-last ball of the day to mid-wicket with nothing more on his mind than seeing out the next and final delivery. But Rick charged down the wicket, thinking of a single, only to realize to his and Peter's horror that Peter was anchored on his bat. Meawhile, Ian Botham swept on the ball and returned it to bowler Miller as Rick scampered back, failing to make his ground by a considerable distance. That dismissal was nothing more than inexperienced cricket at a vital time. I was not very happy about such a wasteful exit for a batsman who was seeing and striking the ball so confidently and well. We were 4–60, and that was disastrous: the ball wasn't all that old; the wicket was still playing tricks; and the England attack, after only one session in the field, had a night to gather their resources and assault us in the morning.

And that they did. Just twenty-five minutes into the third morning Gary Cosier, on 4, tried to drive a Willis delivery. But his edge sailed to Graham Gooch at third slip, and we were 5–78. John Maclean lasted only three minutes for a duck when he tried to sweep a Miller off-spin delivery but edged it from bat to glove to pad and eventually to silly point where Gooch accepted another catch. At 6–79 we needed another 31 runs to avert a follow-on.

Bruce Yardley joined Toohey, who was combating spin and pace alike with competence. He decided that he would chance his arm, as is his vogue whenever possible, and hope that Toohey could do the rest. They took the score to exactly 100 before Yardley tried to club Mike Hendrick's second ball of the day, only to give an edge to wicketkeeper Taylor. His 12 in the partnership of 21 in forty-five minutes went most of the way to averting the follow-on, and Rodney Hogg put that problem behind us before lunch. But at 7–121 at the break we still had an enormous fight on our hands.

Toohey, who scored only seven runs in the opening half-hour, realized at this stage that he had to have a fling in a bid to reduce the huge deficit. Unfortunately, he lost Hogg to a contentious decision when a Willis delivery travelled down the leg side for Taylor to grab it; the end to Hogg's innings of 18 was a blow. Toohey, with sheet-anchor defence from Geoff Dymock at the other end, then opened his shoulders with a succession of pulls and hooks to short-pitched deliveries from Botham. He reached his half-century after 209 minutes and, as he unleashed his renowned cover-drives, cuts, and pulls, our score mounted quickly. The 50 partnership took only sixty-seven minutes and the Englishmen became impatient. Dymock copped a bouncer to show that they had to put up with enough of his broadbat tactics and they were warned by the umpires. Before each Test Mike Brearley and I agreed that bouncers should not be bowled at a certain number of un-recognized batsmen, in this case two from each team. Dymock and Hurst in our camp, and Willis and Hendrick in the England team, were classed as non-recognized batsmen. I was disappointed that this gentleman's agreement was broken. I am not criticizing Brearley outright, because he could not control what a particular bowler might do, but hopefully he told his players and then blasted the culprit.

The new ball was due at that stage and the umpires warned Brearley that they did not want any bouncers at Dymock with the new ball. Unfortunately for us, they didn't need to bounce him from further frustration, because Mike Hendrick found a gap between bat and pad and rattled the stumps when Geoff was 11. Geoff's effort to stick with Peter Toohey for seventy-nine minutes in a partnership worth 58 was a fine effort. They took the score to 9–185. But just five runs and seven minutes later, we were al out for 190. Alan Hurst hit a boundary and took a single before he edged a Willis delivery to wicketkeeper Taylor to settle the issue.

Toohey was unconquered on 81 after 269 minutes of initial defence and later aggression in which he hit six boundaries. This was one of his typically stylish innings that produced the form that eluded him in Brisbane. He is a flashy player who likes to drive, and when he is in full flight he can take an attack apart as quickly and de-moralizingly as anyone in the game. He set up our come-back, but we still trailed by 119 runs and we had a had road to hoe to save the game. The Englishmen again showed their class on a seaming wicket, with Willis taking the honours with 5–44 from 18·5 overs, and Hendrick chiming in with 2–39 from 14 overs.

We had quickly parted the England opening batsmen in the three innings so far and I had no fears that we couldn't do it again the last couple of hours of play. And we should have, too. Hogg upset Boycott with a bouncer that rico-cheted off his glove to the boundary, and then we had to suffer an extraordinary decision that kept Boycott at the wicket after we had no doubts that he edged a Dymock delivery to John Maclean while still on 4.

We were jumping for joy and heading for Geoff to con-gratulate him before we realized the appeal was rejected. We just couldn't believe it because there was a distinct deviation, an audible edge 'click', and nothing but bat in sight at the time. That really set us back on our heels, because with their sheet-anchor gone we thought we might be able to make telling inroads into their line-up before stumps to get back into the game. It wasn't to be and we didn't bowl or field too well after that. Perhaps it affected us more than we thought at the time – only experience will remedy that failing. We also missed an opportunity to remove Gooch when he top-edged a Dymock bouncer in and out of Maclean's gloves. So, both remained at the crease at stumps, with Boycott on 23 and Gooch on 26 with the total at 58.

I think we put it all together in our attack and fielding on the fourth day after the rest day. Mike Brearley said at his press conference that he wanted a lead of 400, and you did not really need a calculator to figure out that at the average run-rate of his batsmen during the opening two Tests that would mean they would still be batting on the last day to achieve that target. Still, with this in mind, I wanted the bowlers to concentrate on accuracy and the fieldsmen to short-circuit as many runs as possible to keep the batsmen under pressure. Naturally, the Englishmen had to play more aggressively to reach a 400-run lead at some mid-stage of the fourth day. If we could restrict them long enough and grab a few early wickets I felt we could force them into error. That is exactly what happened: our bowlers did a magnificent job.

Hogg started the ball rolling by trapping Boycott in front of his stumps before the Yorkshire veteran added to his over-night score of 23. England was 1–58. Boycott, now a regular Hogg victim of the l.b.w. dismissal, played back to try to push the ball to mid-wicket and missed. I could not understand his reluctance to leave the crease. Perhaps he thought he had territorial rights to it, because he had batted so long in the first innings and been on the field during our innings and for another two hours and six minutes of this second innings.

The England team pressed on past 200 and we were starting to really struggle when Kim Hughes dropped a second slip chance from Gooch at 35 from Hogg's bowling. But Hogg, after an unsuccessful appeal for l.b.w., ended the right-hander's innings on 43 when he speared an in-cutter into his pads. Just one minute later Mike Brearley had come and gone. Brearley fended at a Hogg delivery outside the off-stump to the first ball, and John Maclean did the rest to send the England skipper packing for a King duck. England was 3–93, with an overall lead of 212, and still a long way short of that required 400.

However, Derek Randall was once again the thorn in our side. He is such an unpredictable player—that he can score quickly with unorthodox shots that make the setting of a field almost impossible. He planted a couple of shots over mid-wicket from the pacemen after the deliveries pitched outside the off-stump, and he threatened to single-handedly carry out his skipper's wishes. But at 45 he was a little too adventurous when he tried to sweep a Yardley delivery from outside off-stump. The resultant bat-pad edge gave Gary Cosier an easy grab at short leg.

Gower contributed only 12 before he attempted a cut from a Hogg delivery just after lunch; instead, his edge sailed to Maclean, to leave England 4–151. Hard-hitting Ian Botham then slammed four boundaries in an innings of 30 in fifty-three minutes before he spooned Wood a catch at mid-off when slicing a Yardley delivery. England was then in a minor predicament at 6–176. Its lead of 295 was not commanding, because almost five sessions remained for us to get the runs if we could rout them.

Geoff Miller and John Lever therefore took their time and accumulated runs. Miller, becoming a nuisance for us with his constant handy scores late in the batting order, picked up 25 runs in eighty minutes, and Lever 10 in forty-seven minutes, to take the score to 201 before both fell at that score. Lever edged a Hurst delivery to Maclean and then Miller lofted a Yardley delivery to Peter Toohey at mid-wicket. The innings then folded quickly. Taylor, using a runner because of a pulled groin muscle, fell to the second new ball when he edged a Hogg delivery to the wicket-keeper, and Dymock wrapped it up when he bowled Mike Hendrick between bat and pad for 1. A job well done, I thought. England was dismissed for 208 and restricted to a lead of 327, with more than 500 minutes remaining in the match for us to get the runs if we were good enough. Certainly, it was a viable contract.

Admittedly, the England batsmen were out for quick runs. But we did not let them have their way and our persistent, accurate bowling and snappy fielding was a sign that we were learning what Test cricket is all about and, what's more, showing we were capable of doing the job at hand. That man Rodney Hogg had done it again – 5–57 from 17 overs, to give him 10–122 for the match, in a magnificent display. He gained support from Dymock and Hurst and spinner Bruce Yardley, who captured 3–41 in 16 impeccable overs.

Two uncontrollable ingredients put paid to our real chances of victory within thirty minutes of our innings – the wicket and the weather. The first disadvantage came in the form of a Lever delivery that exploded off the wicket and brought about the dismissal of Rick Darling for 5. The wicket was developing cracks, and this Lever delivery hit one of them and cannoned into Darling's glove before ricocheting all the way to mid-on where Boycott held the catch. It was a brute of a ball and Rick was desperately unlucky to receive it, let alone get out to it.

Then the rain came and washed out the final session, leaving us 1–11 at the close. The torrential downpour was a bitter blow to us, as it deprived us of the time advantage we had and made victory virtually impossible. On the other hand, it gave England every chance to attack without reservation the following day, knowing that we would need a superhuman effort to get the runs and that, even in attempting them, we could not help but take risks. So, rather than facing the target of 317 with nine wickets in hand with 480 minutes to get them, we had our odds reduced to the same target in only 360 minutes. All our good work in bowling England out and restricting their tally was really wasted by the downpour. We needed 52 runs an hour for victory and that really wasn't on, especially as 40 runs an hour was the normal scoring rate in the series so far – just about what we had had at our disposal before the rain.

Before lunch on the final day all of that was academic, as we crashed to 4–80. Kim Hughes reached 12 before he played a cut too close to his body and Gooch snapped up a head-high reflex catch at third slip. This gave Willis his first victim of the innings, and we slipped to 2–36.

Then I tickled a leg-side catch to Taylor behind the stumps from Hendrick's bowling after scoring only 3 in almost an hour, and Peter Toohey was out first ball trying to push a Hendrick outswinger. We were 4–58 and survival was our only thought then. Graeme Wood and Gary Cosier were our last hopes, really, and they had a little luck on their side during that eventful first session. Wood was particularly in favour with Lady Luck. Twice he miscued hooks from Botham's bowling, only to watch Boycott misjudge both attempts at mid-wicket. And, to add insult to injury, Wood miscued again and Boycott finally caught it ... off a Botham no-ball. Cosier, on 4, hit a return-catch

o Mike Hendrick, but the England seamer could not cling
o it in his follow-through.

Lunch came and went, and hopes were still alive that this
pair might stay long enough to ensure a draw. But, when the
tand reached 83, Cosier tried to sweep a Miller delivery off
he stumps and was trapped in front for 47 after 110 minutes in the fray. That dismissal triggered a depressing col-
apse. Just two runs later Wood played at a delivery outside
he off-stump from Lever and, after a prolonged delay,
umpire Tom Brooks signalled him out for a spirited 64 in
our hours. That was one of many decisions that baffled
s during the Test, and it did not meet with the approval of
he West Australian crowd, let alone the people who were
watching on national television. But the damage was done
nd then, in quick succession, Maclean was caught in slip
y Brearley from Miller for 1, and Hogg was bowled by
he off-spinner for a duck. This sent us reeling to 8-147.
Lever then removed Yardley for 7, when an edge was
napped up in slips by Botham, and then finished the Test
y bowling Hurst for 5 to rout us for 161.

You cannot explain away a 166-run defeat easily, especi-
lly after two batting collapses. But I maintained that we
ad the potential and that once we put it together we could
eally shake the Englishmen. That didn't hold much water
ith a lot of people after a seven-wicket loss in Brisbane
nd now this defeat here. But the point was that our bowlers
ere doing well and, as individuals at different times, our
atsmen had each shown the ability to score runs. Kim and
did it in Brisbane but failed here, while Peter Toohey and
Graeme Wood came good in this Test. All we had to do
as get it together at the top of the batting order and, I
elt, we could crack the ice.

Another factor that wrecked us in Perth was the wicket.
t times Willis, Hendrick, Lever (who finished with 4-28
the second innings from 8·1 overs), and Botham were un-
layable. They are extremely hard to combat on a pitch
at is designed to help them. They could not have trans-
orted an English wicket to Perth which would have al-
wed them a better use of their seaming skills.

And, finally, I would like to make mention of Tom

Brooks, who has been a tremendous umpire throughout his career. He left the scene on a sore-and-sorry note when he retired at lunchtime on the final day of the Test. I am just disappointed for his sake and ours that he didn't retire before the Test, because he cost us a great deal with his decisions and lost a lot of credibility himself. Some decisions were not the normally-impeccable Brooks' decisions. At one stage during the game while we were fielding he made a shocking decision in favour of an England batsman. He just walked up to me and said, 'I am sorry that I have mucked this Test up for you', and then just walked off. I didn't know what to say. I just looked at him and felt sorry for the bloke.

I am disappointed that Tom Brooks did not retire a match earlier to save himself and us the embarrassment of the Second Test. Perhaps it took that match for him to realize that retirement was necessary. Anyway, as he said he mucked it up for Australia. And for that I am sorry just as I am that Tom Brooks did not go out of Test cricket with the high credit and reputation that he earned over the years.

5 Still Kicking

The Australian Cricket Board, Mike Brearley, and I all seemed to have troubles before the Third Test in Melbourne. The inaugural Benson & Hedges Cup one-day international match planned for the MCG on Boxing Day was washed out, and that disappointed all concerned. A crowd of about 50,000 was expected at the game; instead, the rain cost the Board an estimated $140,000, both the Australian and England teams valuable match practice, and the public the chance to witness what eventually evolved into a thrilling three-part series.

I had my own worries. I was beginning to think that I was not destined to win a game as captain during the 1978–79 summer. After the Second Test I remained in Perth with Alan Hurst for the Victorian Gillette Cup match against Western Australia. I have never beaten a West Australian team in Perth, and I thought we had them in this game. But they won by 1 run in one of the most exciting games I have ever played in. They clubbed 215 runs in 40 overs and, after Jeff Moss and I carted the bowling all over the field in reply, a victory seemed a formality. But we blew it, and I returned to Melbourne despondent about the whole summer and looking forward to the New Year and a possible change of luck.

Mike Brearley then encountered his own kind of trouble. A couple of days before the Test both the Australian and England teams trained at the MCG, but could not use the nets because the grass was still wet from the recent rains and the wickets were naturally dangerous. But, after his players called it quits for the day, Mike decided to have some extra batting practice to help improve his form. He had young England fast bowler Jon Agnew to help him, but the exercise lasted just two deliveries before a rearing delivery smashed into Brearley's left eyebrow.

He needed six stitches in the cut after being taken to hospital. I was fielding with the lads at the time of the incident and I helped Mike into the rooms. It is amazing how easily a bloke can get hurt. He wasn't hit during the fierce battle in the Ashes battle, yet he copped this in a last-minute casual training session.

The day before the Test I specifically sought out each player and asked for a superhuman effort. I was confident, having seen the flat wicket that was prepared, that we could turn the tables and breathe life back into the series. Defeat would mean the Ashes were out of our reach and that just would not do. We had a newcomer to the team, New South Wales' Allan Border, who had been piling up runs at an impressive rate. He replaced Cosier, the team's vice-captain, who was dropped after only 52 runs at an average of 13 in the opening two Tests. Allan, a stylish left-hander, clinched his place with 135 against Western Australia and 114 against Victoria in consecutive innings in the Shield competition. Also, leg-spinner Jim Higgs returned to play on his home ground, where he bowls so well. All-rounder Phil Carlson, twelfth man for the opening two Tests, was left out of the twelve this time, and Bruce Yardley took over the role as drinks waiter.

The toss was vital for this Test. The wicket was flat and dry and likely to get more difficult to score on as the game progressed. In other words, whoever won the toss and batted had every chance to slip into a winning position and clinch the game. For the third time Mike called incorrectly and, gratefully, I told him we would pad up and bat.

More than 35,000 fans flocked to the MCG for that opening day. The support may have stirred on Graeme Wood and Rick Darling, for they were like frisky two-year-olds as they scampered up and down the wicket tempting fate. But their tactics proved effective – even if there were a few close-calls that had everybody gasping for breath – and as both players began to unleash a range of drives, cuts, and pulls the score breezed past 50 in a promising start. Inevitably, the run-out came, however, to finish the union at 65. Wood hit a delivery firmly to Boycott at mid-on and Rick Darling started off head-down for a single. But he was turned back and couldn't make good his ground. That was a frustrating end to a solid start as Darling departed for 33 in little more than an hour and a half.

The running between wickets was not safe all summer and Graeme Wood has to take much of the blame for that, despite a few unlucky incidents that befell him. I think that he is just learning what running between wickets is all about. He wasn't considering his partner at the start of the summer, and that was not a good attitude. Instead of making sure that both he and his partner were guaranteed a single, he would often leave the decision until too late and, if he changed his mind, would unwittingly leave his partner stranded. We lost too many wickets, especially important wickets at the top of the order, during the summer, and Wood undid much of his good work because of this fault.

That run-out was doubly costly because, while on 65 still, we lost Kim Hughes. He played forward to a delivery from Ian Botham before he had scored and was adjudged caught behind for a duck. Suddenly we were 2–65 and that fine start was reduced to a more moderate status.

As I joined Wood I felt that this was a time to attack the bowling as we had from the start, and not fall into a defensive mood that would allow the England bowlers to wrest the initiative. Graeme continued in a support role. His sheet-anchor tactics, sprinkled with an occasional drive and pull, made the Englishmen toil in unusual frustration while I got on with the job of scoring runs. I felt in good form, hitting the ball crisply and for a change realizing that the England seamers were not about to make the ball dart wherever they pleased off the seam. This was our ballgame on a wicket more suited to our style of batting, and that is the way we played. We skipped past the 100 in good time. And, as I took on the bowling with relish, to reach 41 in eighty-two minutes with four boundaries, I felt we were on the path to a tremendous total. But at that moment I edged a Botham delivery to slips where Mike Hendrick held the chance. I was disgusted with myself, because I simply played the wrong line at a time when I had my eye in and everything going for me. As I left the MCG arena we were 3–126 and needing to keep up the attack and retain the initiative. Wood and Toohey did that well, combining for a 63-run partnership in three hours. The Englishmen bowled a professional line and length making us fight for our runs as the field deepened and the pressure was applied. The

59

responsibility was on Wood and Toohey to build the innings, because only Test new chum Allan Border followed what had been a fragile lower order so far in the series.

Toohey was just hitting his straps when he was dismissed, the victim of a miraculous catch by Derek Randall at mid-on. Toohey jumped into a delivery from spinner Miller and hit the ball firmly, and not that far off the turf, for what seemed destined for the boundary. But Randall, an uncanny fieldsman, hurled himself to his left in a desperate bid to stop the ball. And, hey presto, it stuck. A cruel blow that was, because Toohey, following his 81 not out in Perth, was in the right frame of mind to take on this tiring attack on a wicket that was ideal for him. So we were 4–189, and England immediately put every ounce of pressure on young Allan Border. But the twenty-four-year-old ignored the cluster of fieldsmen around the bat and showed great maturity. He was a little nervous early, but once he opened his shoulders and clubbed a Miller delivery over mid-on to the boundary he was away, and loving every minute of it.

Meanwhile Graeme Wood pressed relentlessly towards a century but, with Border surprisingly in control and putting the bowlers through the mill, he did not look as though he would get to his milestone before stumps. As it was, Wood made it in the dying moments of the day. What a tremendous innings it was. He provided the backbone of the innings throughout the day, without forgetting the need for runs. He gladly played second-fiddle to the other batsmen and kept the score ticking along with six boundaries and a host of singles and safely struck twos and threes.

Graeme Wood is one of the best hookers I have seen, but he is not a great driver. He dabs a lot of runs but he is most effective. Importantly, he has the ability to occupy the crease for long periods, overcoming the new ball and paving the way for batsmen down the order. Once he sorts out his running between wickets he will be a more accomplished player and a great contributor to the Test team.

The first day yielded 243 runs for the loss of only four wickets and I was looking for a score approaching 400 to really put pressure on the England batsmen. But after all that good work we had no support from our tailenders, losing 6–15 in an extraordinary turn of events the following morning. The pathetic display took only seventy-five minutes, during which we lost 5–5 at one stage.

Allan Border was the first victim, edging a Hendrick delivery to Brearley at first slip after adding only a boundary to his overnight score. That left us 5–247, and three runs later came the important blow when Wood played a drive to John Emburey at short mid-off from Miller, to depart for an even 100 – again not having added to his overnight score. Then it was a procession. Hogg hit a Miller delivery to Randall in the covers to depart for a duck; Dymock was bowled for Hendrick for a similar total; and Hurst suffered the same fate just two minutes later.

Three ducks in twenty minutes and we were 9–252. John Maclean then played over a yorker from Botham when 8 and our innings was completed for 258. Botham, Miller, and Hendrick shared the bowling honours with three wickets apiece. We had no batting honours that dismal day. I felt real anger and agony about the collapse, because we had thrown away a golden opportunity to build a match-winning score that would give England no hope, and allow us to dictate terms for the rest of the Test.

I told the players, too. I was disgusted at their lack of resistance and let them know before we went out to bowl. They had to redeem themselves.

The reaction was fantastic. Rodney Hogg, with the crowd chanting 'Hoggy – Hoggy' as he charged in to bowl at Boycott, generated awesome speed. The crowd had a marvellous effect on our bowlers. They sat under signs of 'Borecott' to show their disgust with Geoff's batting run rate and waved Australian flags in encouragement. Mike Brearley, who decided to open the batting despite his head injury, must have thought he was back in India or the West Indies as he and Boycott were booed on to the ground.

Suddenly, all hell broke loose. Hogg stormed in for his second over and splayed Boycott's stumps with a glorious inswinger that nipped between the Yorkshireman's bat and pad. Boycott bowled for 1. The crowd went mad, exploding into thunderous applause for Hogg – and then deafening boos for Boycott as he walked grim-faced from the arena.

I thought the stands were going to collapse a couple of deliveries later when Hogg trapped Brearley in front of his stumps for 1 to have England 2–3. Umpire Max O'Connell, who umpired in the Centenary Test here, said that the noise at that stage was far louder than anything he had experienced. I don't doubt it.

Hogg's ability to break the opening stand was amazing. And his dominance over Boycott and Brearley was becoming only too evident. Hogg had claimed Boycott's scalp on five occasions during the summer, including three of the five innings in a Test – and one of those other dismissals was a run-out. And Brearley had now fallen to Hogg for a duck and 1 in his past two innings.

The first session ended with England 2–8 in reply to our 258, and much of our early morning gloom disappeared. The warning had to be made, however, that we had England 2–3 in Perth and that they went on to score 309. So we set out after lunch with a singleminded determination to ram home the advantage this time. Hogg's onslaught was temporarily halted when Jim Higgs missed a short-leg catch from Randall just after the interval. Randall, still on 2, gloved a kicking delivery just five balls into the second session and Higgs, although wrapping his hands around it, could not hold it. That miss set us back a bit and Lady Luck did not smile on us for a while. Randall played and missed often enough, and when he finally did get an edge to a Dymock delivery, it fell short of Border in second slip. But, while still on 13, Randall's luck ran out and ours returned. The fidgety right-hander shuffled across his crease to a Hurst delivery and was trapped in front of his stumps. England was 3–40 and Hurst reaped the reward for nine tidy overs that cost him only 16 runs.

There was suddenly a rout in the air, and everybody sensed it. Hurst rapped Gooch on the pads when he was 24 but could not convince the umpire. Then the lion-hearted Victorian found the outside of David Gower's flashing bat and, unluckily, the ball flew between third slip and gully to the fence to bring up the 50 in 126 anxious minutes. We persisted. Obviously the English batsmen were making heavy weather of the situation under the full force of our pressure. Dymock provided the break that allowed us to penetrate the middle-order when he found the outside edge of Gooch's bat when the beefy right-hander was 25. The ball flew to Border at second slip where, after juggling the ball, he clutched a brilliant catch as he fell on his back. England was in real trouble at 4–52, with only Gower and Botham to save their sinking ship.

Everybody lifted themselves. Rick Darling and Graeme Wood were exceptional in the outfield, the slips were suddenly holding anything that looked like a chance, and the bowlers had full support. Botham was making hard work of the battle, but Gower unfortunately was in the type of mood that earned him his Perth century. He was particularly harsh on Jim Higgs, accounting for all 17 runs from the leg-spinner's bowling before the tea break. He played pulls and cuts and a cover drive with nonchalant ease. He was one of the few players in the opening two sessions who showed any real confidence. Those dramatic 240 minutes saw ten wickets fall for only 90 runs as England took a respite at 4–75.

The last session was again to be ours. Geoff Dymock started the ball rolling when he trapped Gower in front of his stumps for 29 to give us the all-important wicket. England was 5–81, and there was more carnage to come. Higgs, who has the better of Botham, forced the big hitting right-hander to miscue a cover drive: Darling held a fine diving catch to account for the last England recognized batsman, for 22 with the total on 100.

England in fact lost 3–1 as a result of Higgs' wicket, because Hogg returned and rattled the stumps of both Bob Taylor (0) and John Emburey (3), before stumps came with England tottering at 8–107. The bowling reaped rewards it deserved because it was fast, accurate, and directed to the field. Hogg, with 4–24 from 13 overs for the day, once again spearheaded the attack, and it was plain that the Englishmen did not fancy his speed or movement.

England added a further 36 runs the next morning before folding for 143. One interesting aspect of the latter part of their innings was the performance of Geoff Miller. He batted for 125 minutes for 7 runs before he was finally bowled by Hogg. The point was rather obvious to us : you have to make runs while you can because the bowling and the wicket will get you sooner or later. Deliveries were beginning to run along the ground or jump occasionally, and it was only a matter of time before you received the unplayable ball. Hogg, meanwhile, continued his habit of capturing five wickets in an innings. This time he returned the fine analysis of 5–30 from 17 overs to ensure a 115-run lead for our batsmen to capitalize on.

Rick Darling and Graeme Wood probably made the difference for us in this Test, because they followed up their first innings 65-run partnership with a 55-run stand in the second innings. While England could not get a start, we were off-and-running in both innings to set up the middle-order players after the new-ball bowlers had run their race. Not only were Darling and Wood occupying the crease, they were scoring impressively and quickly and had the Englishmen on the retreat with intelligent and aggressive batting. Darling was our first casualty after lunch at 21, when Randall lunged forward in the covers to hold a drive from Miller's bowling. Kim Hughes then took over from Rick in the bid for quick runs until he lost Graeme Wood for 34 with the score at 2–81. Graeme tried to sweep a Botham full-pitched delivery and lost his leg-stump.

I wanted to score our runs as quickly as possibly in the second innings for a number of reasons. As I have already said, there was no point poking about because, sooner or later, one delivery was going to play tricks and bring about your downfall. Secondly, we were not certain of the weather and we wanted to ensure we were not left short of time in the event of rain to dismiss England a second time. And, thirdly, we knew England would be happy to block out the rest of the Test for a draw. So we had to have as much time as possible to dig them out if necessary.

Accordingly, Kim and I were on the lookout for runs, stealing sharp singles if the field were deep, and trying to hit over the top if they advanced. The score rolled along to 101, just before tea, and then I inexcusably went out. I tried to cut a delivery from Miller that jumped a little, and the top edge eased snugly into Bob Taylor's gloves behind the stumps. We were still coasting with a lead of 216, and I instructed Peter Toohey to keep the score rolling along. He played his role to perfection and raced to 20 in half an hour after tea before he lofted an on-drive to see Botham pluck in a super diving catch from Emburey's bowling. Peter was rather unlucky because he fell to an equally fine catch in the first innings. His exit left us 4–136 and, soon after, we lost Allan Border without addition to the score. Allan was the victim of a smart piece of close-to-the-wicket fielding by Mike Hendrick. He turned an Emburey delivery off his toes and was only a pace down the wicket in executing the shot. But he could not retrieve his ground as Hendrick, at silly leg-slip, underarmed the ball into the stumps to run him out.

Kim Hughes took his score to 48 before he jumped down the wicket to Ian Botham and presented Gower in the covers with a simple catch. His innings was full of fine shots, highlighted by a towering 6 over mid-wicket from Miller's off-spin. Hogg managed only 1 run before he was bowled by Botham and, at stumps, we were 7–163. The tail didn't give a yelp the next day as John Maclean, Geoff Dymock, and Jim Higgs all fell with the score on 167.

England needed 283 for victory with better than five sessions to play : a fair enough contract, except for the wicket and Rodney Hogg. Once again we were away to a flying start that put England behind the eight-ball in no uncertain terms. Dymock beat Brearley outside the off-stump, and the hapless England skipper headed for the pavilion for a duck as Maclean accepted the catch. Brearley's venture as an opening batsman was a flop. His efforts of 1 and 0 gave him only 37 runs in six innings and he must have been thanking the Gods that he was captain of All England and that his place in the team could be saved by virtue of that fact.

England's plight at 1–1 worsened to 2–7, just a few minutes later, when Hogg pinned Randall in front of the stumps. Randall, the bogey man of Brisbane, was out for only 2. I felt then that any thoughts England might have had about a carefree run-chase went back into the saddened pavilion with him. The game now was a matter of England blocking and Australia trying to dig them out. Boycott, relishing the situation, found a willing ally in

Gooch, and the labour was on in earnest.

What was I saying? Maybe Graham Gooch did not get the message because, although Boycott played his stonewall game to perfection, Gooch started to cut loose with resounding results. He clubbed a couple of boundaries and, with Boycott nudging runs here and there, the score slipped past 30, 40, 50, and then 60. As Gooch, solid in defence and ruthless with five boundaries to anything that was loose, began to gain momentum, we became concerned about breaking the union. Hogg thankfully came to the rescue when he trapped Gooch in front for 40 to end a 65-run partnership that took only an hour and a half. England was 3–71 and we could breathe a little easier.

Gower, an irresistible stroke-maker, decided to pick up the gauntlet. He unleashed several fine cuts and drives to take over from where Gooch left off, and his union with Boycott scooted England past the century and into a sphere where the game was wide open. Gower's dominance enabled he and Boycott to register a half-century partnership, and our fieldsmen had to retreat to stem the run-flow. I always felt that we always had enough runs and that all we really needed was a couple of wickets quickly to put the issue beyond doubt.

Hurst proved the man for the occasion when he pinned Boycott in front of his stumps for 38, after the dour opener had defied us for more than three hours. That was the important wicket, because Boycott's presence gave the more fluent England batsmen a sense of security in that at least one end was safe at all times. Gower had dominated the partnership of 51 runs but now that his 'mentor' – the man who helped him through to his Perth century – was gone, the game took on a completely different complexion. With Gower and Ian Botham at the wicket we had a chance of dismissing either at any time, as both players chance their eye and arm and always give the bowlers a chance to claim their wickets.

The crunch came with the score on 163 when both batsmen finally succumbed. Gower, on 49 in a fighting innings of almost three hours, played back to a Dymock 'scooter' and was found in front of his stumps, while Botham slashed against the spin of Jim Higgs and was caught at the wicket for 10. England was 6–167. From then on it was plain sailing, as Hogg returned to put paid to the tailenders. Higgs, with Botham's scalp under his belt, continued the slide when he had Miller caught by Hughes for 1, and then Hogg dismissed Taylor for 5 when the plucky wicket-keeper edged Maclean a regulation chance.

By stumps the Test was ours – barring rain the following day, which thankfully didn't come – as England tottered at 8–171. Fittingly, Hogg ended the match for us just twenty-four minutes into the fifth day. He rapped Willis on the glove, and I held a reflex catch at short square leg; and then he bowled Mike Hendrick for a duck. That gave him 10–66 from 34 overs for the match, his second successive bag of 10 wickets against England in a fantastic performance. Hogg had 27 wickets in only three Tests, including five wickets in an innings in each of England's five completed innings of the series, and he was besieged by the rest of us and about 10,000 fans who came to watch our final glory. As we left the centre area for the presentations I looked at the scoreboard with a smile. England was out for 179, and that made it a 103-run victory to bring us back to a 2–1 situation in the series.

I was extremely proud of the team effort in this game. The team showed fighting spirit to come back after trailing 2–0 in the series, with nobody giving them any hope of even getting close to beating England (we were 13–2 before the Test). The performance of Rodney Hogg was outstanding, and the work of Alan Hurst and Geoff Dymock was always a menace to the England batsmen.

The batting showed solidarity from the start, where the two half-century opening partnerships made all the difference to our performance. The batting showed that once we put it together as a group of batsmen, rather than as individuals, we were capable of scoring heavily and confidently tackling the England attack. I felt that we showed improvement in Perth and that we had multiplied that improvement in Melbourne on a wicket that was flat and more our style.

This was Australia's first win against England since the Centenary Test here in 1977, and we were extremely proud of that. And I had a special reason to smile. Besides recording my first victory as Australian captain, I had inflicted Mike Brearley's first defeat in sixteen Tests at the England helm. So all eyes turned to Sydney where we began the Fourth Test just three days later.

6 Skinned Alive

All hell broke loose in Sydney before the Fourth Test. We gathered for training at the Sydney Cricket Ground nets on the Thursday afternoon just two days before the all-important match, and that's when it happened. John Maclean was batting in the nets, and Alan Hurst sent him down an ordinary half-volley. John played forward in the normal way and, suddenly, the ball exploded off the wicket and crashed into his left eye. I was watching the whole thing because I was bowling in the same net, and I just could not believe it. The ball had taken a large divot out of the wicket, reared, and given Macca no chance in the world to avoid it. He reeled back, holding his hand to his eye. Alan and I raced up to him. 'I'm gone, I'm gone', he kept saying as we helped him. That's all he could say. Macca had waited a long time to play for his country, and all he could think about was that this accident would keep him out of the Test.

I looked around and there was pandemonium. The Press were there and cameras were flashing. The other players were immediately in to lend a helping hand and, in general, everybody was flustered and upset. I went inside with Macca and tried to ring a doctor without luck. Then a Board representative took Macca to a doctor for stitches and x-rays. Practice was useless after that. For starters, nobody trusted these underprepared wickets and, besides, we were all naturally concerned and upset for Macca.

Fortunately our fears were allayed when the x-rays revealed no breaks and the specialists reported that there would be no permanent damage to the eye. That night I do not think any of the players slept too well.

Macca had six stitches over his left eye and already he had one of the best 'shiners' you could ever imagine. He tried to sleep with ice-packs on his eye, while Alan Hurst (his room-mate) pumped tablets into him to reduce the puffiness and ugly swelling. I spent most of the evening talking to the media. Everyone was naturally interested because we had just won in Melbourne and we were trying to level the series 2-all here. Macca was the vice-captain and the wicketkeeper, and that made him a hard man to replace if necessary. New South Wales wicketkeeper Steve Rixon had just failed a fitness test for an arm injury, so he was out of contention also. The media wanted up-to-the-minute reports on Macca's condition, interviews and pictures of him, of Hurst, comment from me as captain, and 'think stories' on what might happen if Macca didn't play ...

By Friday, on the eve of the Test, Macca still had only a 50–50 chance of playing. But his chances had improved dramatically, and our hopes rose that he might make it to the post. A specialist examined him and ordered another examination before the toss the next day. The selectors also sent out an SOS to Victorian wicketkeeper Ian Maddocks, who joined us that afternoon.

In between all this drama and confusion, we had a couple of functions to attend, training, and massive exposure to the media. I have never been so busy in my life. All the external pressures were beginning to have an adverse effect, and I found it impossible to concentrate on the coming game and build myself up. In short, I needed a manager to handle some of the off-field troubles. Ordering taxis, handling press conferences, and carrying out every other extraneous duty was having a detrimental effect. More was said about that later on in the Tour.

What made it doubly difficult was that there was virtually no time between the Tests. We had just played our hearts out in Melbourne and, with a jet flight, a training run, and a host of incidents we had to shape up again. Naturally, I would prefer about a week between Tests; but I appreciate the finances and holiday periods determine such things and must take preference. Nonetheless, we were all rather jaded. The injury to John Maclean naturally added to our problems.

The Saturday arrived and the drama unfolded. Ian Maddocks was as toey as John Maclean after the specialist gave Macca the all-clear. But he had to get the nod from the selectors, and that took some doing. He put on the gloves and caught a number of balls hit at him. Finally, the verdict came through that he was okay and could take his place in the team. Poor 'Maddo', he was just an hour away from his Test debut, but he took it in good spirit and eventually stayed in Sydney for the match to give us a hand and lend encouragement.

The toss was the next item on the agenda, and I really wanted to win this one and bat. The wicket was absolutely magnificent for the first day, the weather was oppressive and hardly encouraging for fast bowlers and, besides, I would have liked to have given Macca an extra day to recover before he had to stand behind the stumps. No such luck. Mike won his first toss of the series and batted. Well, at least we would have the benefit of any early movement and life in the wicket, I thought, to console myself as I went in to tell the players of the verdict.

We were immediately under pressure when Rodney Hogg bowled only three overs in the heat and had to leave the field, complaining about difficulty in breathing. We were in real trouble, because we had played for fifty-five minutes and England was 18 runs advanced without a loss when Hogg wandered off the field. Alan Hurst and Geoff Dymock really had to put their shoulders to the grindstone if we were to stop England from amassing a huge total. That was the signal for Hurst to step into the breach and take over the star role. He forced Boycott into error and the edge was snapped up in second slip by Allan Border. I felt we had Boycott sorted out pretty well. He likes the glide down between slips and gully – a shot that brings him a lot of runs in England. But he did not get many runs from that pet shot against the new ball in Australia. We would take out one of the slips as I moved into silly point, and I don't think he liked that. He was so busy watching me to see what I was doing that he was unable to think about his own game. He lacked concentration, believe it or not. His concern for my activities generally made him play a rash shot early, or try for that glide to gully. By the number of times he was l.b.w. or caught in the slips you can see that we had him in his own private war.

Boycott's 8 helped England to only 1–18, and Hurst struck again when Derek Randall had faced only his second ball. Randall is susceptible to the hook early, a shot he doesn't play well. He is extremely strong on the pull in front of the wicket, but he does not have control of the hook against the new ball. Hurst bounced him immediately and Randall could not resist it. He tried to hook – and, to be honest, he hit it pretty well – but he succeeded only in clubbing it head high to Graeme Wood at backward square-leg. Out for a duck, and we had England on the run once again at 2–18.

Hogg came back on to the field about thirty minutes later but had to 'serve time' under the rules and, meanwhile, Hurst and Dymock kept the pair of Mike Brearley and Graham Gooch in check. Then Hogg came back into the attack and dismissed Brearley for 17 with the score at 3–35 with a magnificent piece of bowling. Hogg bowled a succession of deliveries short of a length, gradually forcing the England skipper further and further on to the back foot. Then he whipped in a full length 'rocket' that uprooted Brearley's off-stump. We could hardly have asked for more on this fine batting wicket than to have England in this situation, but Hurst had not finished before the luncheon interval. In a lion-hearted effort, Hurst came again to put the icing on the morning play when he found the outside edge of Gower's bat in the last over before lunch. John Maclean accepted the catch to dismiss the left-hander for 7 and send England tumbling to 4–51.

Macca was delighted with the catch but could not wait to get back into the dressing-rooms. We noticed when he took the field at the start of play that he was perspiring profusely. Before a ball was even bowled his shirt was clinging to his back and sweat was streaming down his face. I asked him then if he was all right, and he said that it was just the exhausting weather. But, as the morning session progressed, he became weaker and weaker and the perspiration absolutely flooded from his body. He was obviously suffering from a reaction to the drugs and his actions became slower and slower. He discarded his saturated gear at lunch and changed into new gear. He said he was feeling much better after a shower and was prepared to take the field again.

After the break I introduced Jim Higgs into the attack to give the pacemen a breather. Bowling quickly in the

72

35-degree heat was a monstrous strain on anybody and I had to save each of them for short and sharp spells if possible. This was true of Hogg, particularly, because he was struggling to make it through an over, let alone his usual three. Gooch, meanwhile, was looking anything but dangerous. Although the attack was wilting in the heat, he played a patient innings, possibly waiting for us to melt away completely. That was a mistake on his part, because Higgs beat him with a delivery that spun slightly more than the right-hander expected and Peter Toohey held the catch. Gooch's 18 runs in a total of 5–66 had taken 105 minutes, and he had sacrificed his normally-aggressive game to recoup little reward.

Hurst bounced back into action immediately and struck again, this time inducing Geoff Miller to edge John Maclean a catch behind the stumps after previously edging a boundary through slips for his only runs. I couldn't believe it. England was 6–70 and heading for disaster on a glorious batting wicket. Maybe we had found more cracks in their armour than we thought, or perhaps their confidence was absolutely shot to bits.

Macca by this stage was a wreck. Not long after lunch he came up to me and said he was in trouble, suffering pins and needles in his hands that made it difficult to feel the ball in his gloves. He could not concentrate and was becoming lethargic. I told him to leave the field and head for a doctor if he wasn't well. Nobody wanted him to be a hero if it was going to affect his health. But Macca's effort really was one of a hero. All he kept saying was that it might improve, and that he did not want to let the team down, so he would stick on for as long as possible.

After he held the Miller catch I think he realized that too much was at risk for him to stick on. With England six wickets down he had more than done enough. The following over he simply didn't feel one of Higgs' deliveries go in or out of his gloves. He called me across and said he had to get off the field out of the scorching sun for a rest. I asked the umpires if Macca could retire immediately, and if I could slip on the gloves, and they agreed.

I automatically took the gloves because I was the most 'experienced' bloke in the side apart from Macca as a wicket-keeper. I had kept wickets occasionally at Carey Grammar in my school days and also for Walsall in England. I wasn't a raw recruit then, and I knew that if I didn't shape up I could always give Rick Darling a chance because he was also not a novice at the job.

I never visualized that one day I would be wicketkeeping for my country and I found the task challenging and exciting. Hogg bowled a couple that banged into my gloves and a few that did not. I appreciated then the dramatic change of pace he had, and also the enormous concentration a wicket-keeper needs. You have to give your full attention to every delivery, picking up the pace, the line, and the length. Unlike even in slips, the pressure is enormous. You have to take the ball – which I might add is not as easy as it looks – and you are more likely to be the one to have to go for the catch from a thin edge. I do not think I would be exaggerating if I said that I wanted Hogg to just knock over the stumps and do it on his own.

Fortunately I had a chance to get my eye in because, while Ian Botham decided that the England collapse had no bearing on his hard-hitting style, the next two wickets didn't need my assistance. Before England reached 100, Bob Taylor and John Emburey fell to Jim Higgs. Taylor, after contributing 10, deflected a catch to Allan Border in slip, and then Emburey failed to score. England was 8–98. Botham had support from Bob Willis – a master at planting his long leg down the track and padding away the spinners – and he passed his half-century and pressed on to 59.

Then I took my first – and possibly my last – wicket as a 'keeper for Australia. But it was one to remember, even if it was not all that difficult. Botham tried to hook a Hogg bouncer and he managed only to send me a top-edge. You do not have time to even think 'Hell, I've got to hold this', because it comes so quickly. Anyway, I grabbed it, held it in the air, and shouted with real enthusiasm as Botham left the scene. Botham's innings was full of brute power, many punishing drives, and a large slice of responsibility. He was there for only 144 minutes for his 59, and he helped the score move from 4–51 to 9–141 when he finally departed. Alan Hurst then fittingly wrapped up the innings when he bowled Mike Hendrick for 10, giving him fantastic figures of 5–28 from 10·6 overs in that oppressive heat. Jim Higgs also bowled ideally, keeping it tight and collecting 3–42 from 18 overs. Hogg, despite his absence, chipped in with 2–36 from 11 overs, and England was out for 152 after only 52·6 overs.

This was our best effort, I felt, for the series. We had nothing going for us. The wicket was ideal for batting, the heat was oppressive, Hogg had to leave the field after only three overs and did not make his normal early inroads, and then Hurst and Higgs put up superhuman performances. And John Maclean was off the field too. The Englishmen deserved a real caning for their woeful batting, but they did not get it from the media. Apparently, there was a general belief that the wicket was poor from the start of the game and that excused the Englishmen's performance. Certainly there had been an enormous amount of traffic on the SCG before this Test, with both Shield and WSC matches. But this first-day track really was a gem. It did not stay that way, but on the first day no batsman could have asked for more. So, we did not get much credit, and the Englishmen did not get a blast.

Even the fact that we ended the day at 1–56 in only sixty-seven minutes from 12 overs apparently did not sway that strange opinion of the wicket. How I would have loved to have batted there all day. Our innings admittedly did not start too well when Bob Willis bowled Melbourne century-maker Graeme Wood for a duck. But that really was bad luck, because Wood played the ball on to his stumps when engaged in a comfortable defensive shot.

Rick Darling was the man of the moment from then on as he sent drives, cuts, and particularly pulls to the boundary on six occasions to reach 35 not out. The Englishmen played to his hook, thinking that he would miscue and get out as had been his wont throughout the summer. But the wicket had nothing in it for pacemen, and the ball sat up nicely for Rick to select the picket on the fence before he hit the ball. Kim Hughes also picked up two boundaries in his unbeaten 15. We were sitting pretty, only 96 runs in arrears with nine wickets in hand, at the end of the opening day.

John Maclean, having showered and relaxed and off the

tablets that affected him, recovered well overnight. So he joined us on the Sunday in the rooms as we watched the Englishmen toil in the blistering sun. Our first-wicket partnership realized 125 runs in 183 minutes as we took toll of the England attack with a vengeance. Rick Darling was in magical form, while Kim Hughes played sensibly to ensure a big first innings lead. The 50 partnership came in an hour together, and the 100 partnership was also in good time. With Bob Willis indisposed with heat exhaustion we had plenty going for us, especially as Rick Darling and Kim Hughes made the spinners John Emburey and Geoff Miller pay dearly for any loose deliveries.

But with the total at 126 Kim was caught by Emburey as Willis returned to the attack. Kim hit six boundaries in his 48 and ensured a good total for us, after coming in with the score at 1–1 and forcing the Englishmen into retreat. I went to the wicket determined to keep on the pressure and retain the initiative. Rick slipped past his half-century by this stage and was well on the way to his century. Everything looked rosy.

Rick was playing a mature innings, satisfying himself to wait for the loose deliveries to club and determined to make the bowlers bowl to him rather than allow them to make him chase their deliveries. So we breezed into a first-innings lead and I was hitting the ball well, while Rick moved into the 90s. Then our game fell apart. Geoff Miller enticed Rick to turn a delivery around the leg corner – he actually hit it well – but Ian Botham snapped up a low reflex catch. Not many cricketers I know would have held it, but that is beside the point. Rick headed back to the pavilion naturally disappointed that he had missed a century that everybody agreed he deserved.

Rick's demise left us 3–178, and that was quickly converted to 4–179 just five minutes later. Peter Toohey fended at a rising delivery from Botham after scoring only a single, and his thick edge flew to Graham Gooch at third slip-cum-gully where the hefty fieldsman held a sharp chance. That was a blow, because at this stage in the day I was hoping that Peter's flashing blade might have carved up the bowling and set us up completely. That wasn't to be. Allan Border joined me and, at that point, while still wanting as many runs as possible, we had to play a little more cautiously lest we collapsed. The score moved past 200 comfortably enough, and we were back on top, when I was out for 44. Mike Hendrick bowled me a lifting ball outside the off-stump, and I cut it firmly but late. Botham threw out his left hand from third slip and it stuck. After hitting five boundaries I was feeling good after two hours in the centre and I cursed that man Botham as I left the field. He is worth three men in that side at times. He top-scored with a brazen half-century in their innings, accounted for Toohey, and also held two fine catches to remove Rick Darling and me.

At 5–210 and a lead of only 58 we needed solid batting and resistance from the middle-order which so far had been lacking, particularly as the middle-order became latter-order. But we failed in that department once again. John Maclean managed only a dozen runs before he was trapped in front by Emburey with the total at 235, and then Rodney Hogg was run out for 6 in a waste of a wicket. Only Border showed the spirit that was demanded in the situation – he remained unbeaten on 31 after two and a half hours at the crease. At stumps then we were 7–248, a lead of only 92, after being in a super position at mid-afternoon. After being 2–178 we lost 5–70 against a tired, depleted attack in depressing heat. I would not criticize our scoring rate, because it was hot for the batsmen as well as the bowlers, and we had to use every ounce of effort to concentrate while in the middle. After being in the sun most of the previous day I think we felt the effects while we were batting on the second day. I have never played in a match where the weather has been so hot. It was 35 degrees every minute of the day and the humidity was exhausting. But, that aside, our middle-order did not bat well and let us down. Full credit must go to the Englishmen, for they did not budge an inch despite our early batting success. Their fightback later in the day was what Test cricket is all about.

Our tail folded for another 46 runs the next day, and we were dismissed for 294, a lead of 142. Border carried the bulk of the responsibility and was left marooned on an unbeaten 60 in an innings of great maturity that included four boundaries in four hours. More's the pity that he ran out of partners, because he was hitting the ball crisply and firmly and was in no trouble whatsoever. But Geoff Dymock (5 in sixty-six minutes) and Jim Higgs (11 in forty minutes) could do little more than stay at the crease for as long as possible. The real blame had to be levelled at our middle-order that collapsed the previous day.

Jackpot. We started our bid for victory in a sensational way when Rodney Hogg trapped Geoff Boycott in front of his stumps with the first ball of the second innings. Rodney just ambled in and sent down a medium-paced 'loosener' that Boycott played back to defensively, missed, and was struck below the knee. I do not know who was most surprised – Hogg, Boycott, or the rest of us. That was real celebration material, because Boycott was the type of player I thought would relish the situation and block us for hours and hours as he had in Perth.

That dismissal – believed to be Boycott's first in Test cricket first ball – sparked a bit more controversy than normal. Actually there was no doubt about the l.b.w. decision. It was the aftermath that caused feathers to fly. Boycott was walking up the steps to the pavilion when there was apparently a cross-fire between he and a member, who turned out to be a politician. There were public apologies demanded by the MP, silence from Boycott, and eventually the whole thing counted for nought – exactly Boycott's score, and the England total after just one minute.

Then came the decision that swung the whole course of the Test. Geoff Dymock bowled from the northern end just before lunch to Derek Randall when he was just off the mark. It pitched middle and kept low, and there is no doubt it would have missed the leg-stump, and the off-stump. But it would have knocked the middle-stump out of the ground half-way up the stick. 'Not out' was the response to our jubilant appeal. Honestly, I did not realize the umpire had made that extraordinary decision until I was just about twenty metres up the wicket ready to kiss Dymock on the cheek – so convinced was I and the rest of the players behind the stumps that this made Boycott's l.b.w. decision look like a wide ball. That decision changed the course of the match, as I said. Instead of winning by anything as convincing as an innings or ten wickets we were back in a struggle.

I do not want to give the impression that I am criticizing the umpire for costing us that opportunity to coast to victory. But what I will say is that this particular verdict which went against us at an important time just before lunch was typical of the many that put us behind the eight-ball throughout the summer. As I said at the start of the book, normally these things level out. And this one did ... about 150 runs later after Randall had put England right back into the game.

The galling part was that even Randall, who rarely concedes he is out unless his three stumps are pinned to the sight-screen, said to us and his team-mates later that he was the luckiest guy in the world and, if he was ever going to walk for an l.b.w., that would have been it. Blimey, was I hostile about that. It really made me feel heaps better, I can tell you. Randall and Brearley opened out after lunch and, as the heat took its toll once again, we could not maintain the pressure. Randall, with a hook, a cover-drive, and an on-drive, looked menacing while Brearley came out of his shell for the first time in the series with a couple of fine off-drives. They blunted our every aggressive move and thrashed anything that was remotely loose to reach a century partnership late in the day. I was at my wits' end to try to break the stand. Higgs was operating from one end and causing a few anxious moments to both players without luck, while I rotated Hogg, Hurst, and Dymock in three-over spells from the members' end – again without a sniff of a breakthrough. In desperation, I brought on Allan Border to give the pacemen a breather, and because the wicket was beginning to take unpredictable spin. One delivery would come straight through, and the next might jump and turn. I thought his left-arm orthodox deliveries might do the trick.

Allan is only a part-time spinner but he can bowl on a spot and that's all that was really needed. With the score at 111 (Lord Nelson really has the wood on these Englishmen) Brearley casually pushed forward to what seemed another regulation delivery and was shocked to hear that deadly rattle of ball hitting stumps. The ball spun and scooted, and that was Brearley's lot after a solid 53 in 217 minutes of a partnership of 111. We had thirty-seven minutes left to capitalize on the situation, but Randall lashed out for another 16 runs in that time while Graham Gooch picked up 6. At stumps England was 2–133, and still nine runs in the red.

Randall was still there on 65 after 254 minutes, much to our disgust. Besides that lucky escape, he constantly annoyed us as he pulled away when a bowler – particularly a fast bowler – was in his run-up. He would wander towards the umpire and ask for some flyspray, oblivious to the rest of the game. I had words with him about this a couple of times, because it was hot enough in the centre in 40-degree heat without having our bowlers wasting energy running half-way to the wicket only to see the batsman meander in the direction of square leg. I suppose there is a place in cricket for a guy like Randall. But, honestly, he is hard to cop at times. He chats to himself all the time and seems to have an idea that when he is batting everything and everybody must operate according to his whims: for example, the flyspray stunt. When somebody has a shot at him about it he is horrified, wondering why we are upset. Strange man, this.

Perhaps a few of our batsmen should try it, because his asides probably only upset us while he went from strength to strength the fourth day. After taking half an hour to score his first run he slipped into top gear and never gave us a look-in. He and Gooch took the score to 150 and a lead in 314 minutes, but we claimed our first joy with the score at 169. Higgs, who switched from the outer to the members' end, forced Gooch into a bat-pad error and Graeme Wood took a reflex catch at silly mid-off. Gooch's contribution was 22 in 130 minutes, and his dismissal left England only 27 in front with three of their topline batsmen out of action. But David Gower decided to put as wide a space between England and our score as quickly as possible when he reached the wicket, and he clubbed 18 runs in swift time before lunch.

Randall, 87 at lunch, again took time to settle in and I maintained the spin of Jim Higgs for as long as possible before taking the second new ball. The 200 had come and gone after 82 overs and, with Jim feeling the pinch a little after a long stint, I took the new ball two overs later. I was reluctant to do so because I feared the bouncier and harder new ball would make scoring on this flat wicket far easier. The wicket was for spin, not speed.

Unfortunately, my fears turned to reality as Randall blasted his way through the 90s with three boundaries from four deliveries from Hogg. That registered his 100 after 411 minutes at the wicket, and gave him his second century in twenty Tests for England – his other being, of course, that 174 in the Centenary Test against Australia. I congratulated him as I walked past and thought I might have a dig at the same time. 'Why don't you come in for a drink after stumps, seeing you have done so well', I suggested to him. He was stunned and could not reply. As I mentioned earlier, few of the Englishmen worried about that sort of hospitality usually, and Randall could not quite figure that one out. A lot of people think that Randall likes to talk during his innings because it helps him concentrate. I don't agree in one regard. He will certainly talk to anyone who will listen, but I do not think he likes having questions put to him. If you ask him a few curly questions while he is there, he tries to figure out an answer – and he cannot be concentrating while he is doing that.

He lost concentration just after his century but, luckily for him, a few lofted drives lobbed out of reach of our fieldsmen and a few lusty swings did not connect. Then, alas, he settled down again. Meanwhile, Gower scooted to 34 from 68 deliveries and was on the warpath until he edged a Hogg delivery to Maclean behind the stumps. I was pleased to see the back of him, because I regard him as the best batsman in the England camp by a long way, with Randall the second best. England was 4–237 at that point and, with Botham the only recognized batsman to follow and a lead of only 95 with the new ball only eight overs old, England turned to stone-wall tactics once again. Our next success for the day came an hour and a half later, after Botham had painstakingly worked his way to 6. He was tied in knots by Higgs and the break finally came for the workhorse of the day when he deceived Botham, who presented Wood with a catch when the score was 5–267. Randall, like Ol' Man River, just kept flowing along, and I thought we would never run him dry. He and Miller added another 25 runs before the Gods finally smiled on us. Hogg forced Randall on to the back foot and the little right-hander missed and paid the consequences. 'Hoorah', I shouted. After 589 minutes we had him. I did not think much of his first dig in this innings, but his second was a masterly piece of batting. His concentrated effort had taken England from 1–0 to 6–292 when he departed, and he had amassed 150 of them. It was an innings I will never forget for several reasons.

By stumps England was 6–304 and holding a lead of 162. We had put down five catches to make life difficult for ourselves in oppressive conditions, and we still had to remove a couple of batsmen renowned for occupying the crease before we could set out after victory on the final day. The honours in the bowling went unchallenged that day to Jimmy Higgs. He returned 2–123 from a marathon fifty overs, but that analysis of wickets gives a totally phoney picture of his effort. He bowled his heart out, found the edge on countless occasions – having three of them put down and a couple more passing untouched between the wicketkeeper and his two slips – and generally had the batsmen in all sorts of trouble without them being good enough to get out. Hogg's 3–64 were statistically the best, and he too was unlucky on several occasions.

Higgs and Hogg shared the spoils on the last day as we had to wait another important 42 runs and eighty-two minutes to wrap up the England second innings. Hogg stepped in to split the Miller-Taylor union after twenty minutes when he trapped Miller in front for 17. Then Higgs took over, removing Emburey (14) and Willis (0) with consecutive deliveries, and wrapping up proceedings by courtesy of a Toohey slips catch to dismiss Hendrick for 7. Taylor remained 21 not out in an important innings that lasted 110 minutes. That deprived us of time besides giving us those extra few runs to score.

Higgs richly deserved his bag of 5–148 from a mountainous 59·6 overs, while Hogg finished with 4–67 to keep him on the road to a series record. Higgs' fingers and right hand were so limp that night he could hardly hold a beer, and little wonder.

The contract was 205 runs in 265 minutes on a wicket that was taking considerable spin. But the challenge had to be taken up for us to level the series 2-all.

Rick Darling and Graeme Wood gave us a flying start with 38 runs in fifty-one minutes. Mike Brearley was on the retreat as his field spread towards the boundaries as the pair cut and pulled vigorously to anything short and took risks against the new ball. But Rick, when 13, played defensively to a Hendrick leg-cutter and saw Gooch take a fine diving catch low to his right in gully. Kim Hughes went to the wicket with the intention of clubbing the spinners Emburey and Miller out of the ground. Indeed, a couple of lusty hits, and mis-hits, had Brearley switching his field furiously. But then came the turning point in our innings – yet another inexcusable run-out. Wood, doing nicely as he moved to 27 from sixty-four deliveries, pushed a Miller delivery into the covers and called for a single. He charged down the wicket, but Kim apparently had not heard him. To both batsmen's horror, they were staring each other in the face at the bowler's end. Botham calmly fielded and, when his return reached Bob Taylor, Wood was the length of the wicket out of his ground with Hughes still anchored to his crease. That pathetic dismissal not only left us at 2–44, but took the wind out of our sails a little and gave the Englishmen every reason to think that we would panic in the run-chase and capitulate.

I came and went for just 1 run, but that was more bad luck than panic or capitulation. Mike Hendrick sent me down a leg-cutter and, as I went to push it back, the ball jumped and hit the handle of my bat and ballooned back to Hendrick on his follow-through.

Mike Hendrick had 2–12 from nine overs; besides halting our run rate he had disrupted our top order. That little stint was enough for Brearley to bring his men in close for his spinners, realizing that we were needing better than a run a minute and that we had two new batsmen at the crease who had to settle in before convincing shots could be played.

His spinners Emburey and Miller just bowled a line and

let the wicket do the rest for them. With half a dozen men hovering around the batsmen, only one mistake was needed and that was it. Before we knew what had happened we were shot to bits. Peter Toohey jumped down the wicket to Miller with his head in the air, and was bowled for 5. That wicket followed the dismissal of Hughes for 15 when he played a bat-pad to Emburey from Miller. Suddenly, we were 5–74. I told John Maclean to be careful or England would run all over us. Macca could not do anything about it as he prodded forward to a ball that jumped and he was caught by Botham at silly point for a duck.

That really was it. Allan Border was in fine touch and he blazed away with some cover drives and lofted straight drives, but nobody could stay with him. Geoff Dymock lasted only eight minutes for a duck before Emburey bowled him, and Hogg turned a ball to Botham close to the wicket off the same bowler for a five-minute duck. 8 for 85 and the rest was a formality. Jim Higgs lasted twenty-five minutes with a straight bat before he was adjudged l.b.w. to Emburey for 3, and Alan Hurst was bowled for another duck. Once again Allan Border was marooned on an unbeaten 45 in our only batting bright spot of a disastrous day.

The Ashes would remain with England as they took a 3–1 lead in the series. We were distressed at our performance. I was disgusted. Seven of our last eight batsmen contributed a paltry nine runs between us and, apart from Border, were of no value in what started out as a victory-bid.

We were beaten by 93 runs after managing only 111. That, naturally enough, brought acid criticism from our detractors. The let-down was bad enough. We had this Test in our keeping for four days and then blew it. What's more, we had outplayed England for nine of the last ten match days and still lost the Ashes by coming out of that one-sided battle with a win apiece. As Mike Brearley said later, it was an extraordinary win for his side. From our viewpoint it was an extraordinary loss.

7 Hogg on the Spit

Rodney Hogg ran rampant through the English batsmen during the series and, unfortunately, he tried on several occasions to ride roughshod over me. Adelaide during the Fifth Test was the site for the showdown, in what became popularly known as the Yallop-Hogg Affair. This was no love affair and, in fact, there were plenty of heated words exchanged, on and off the field. At one stage Hogg suggested we survey the back of the Adelaide Oval – and I don't think he had a tennis match on his mind.

The showdown had been brewing for most of the series. I had met Hogg only a couple of times in Melbourne District cricket when he was playing for Northcote and I was representing Richmond. He was a young fast bowler from an opposition camp and really I didn't get to know him at all. So it was not until I reached Brisbane for the First Test that I really had a chance to speak to the guy. Basically, I didn't know him: what he did for a living, where he lived in South Australia, if he was a bachelor, or any of the usual points that a team-mate, let alone a captain, should know about a player in the side.

Our differences of opinion came within an over of England's first innings in the Brisbane Test. He took it upon himself to change the field placings without consulting me. I had never experienced anything like this before and I was just open-mouthed in astonishment. I immediately had a chat with him and suggested that we work out the field placings together, and he agreed to that principle. But within a couple of deliveries he was at it again. He gets so wrapped up in what he is doing that he forgets about everything and takes matters into his own hands. He showed a lack of regard for my position as captain, and apparently believed that while he was bowling everything should centre around him and his wishes.

I believe that a bowler should be happy with his field placings and this is all right up to a point. You cannot have a bowler running the whole side while the captain sits by and watches. Hogg has a lot of ideas about various positions, and I respect them. But I also disagree with a lot of his theory. If I don't think that a particular field placing is in the general interests of the team, I will not buckle to the bowler's request. So we started off on the wrong foot in this regard, and a few minutes later he shocked me again. After only three overs he walked up to me and said he was tired and would not be bowling the next over. He didn't ask if we needed another over from him; he simply threw me the ball and said he had had enough. He is certainly a man of surprises, I thought at the time. But what could I do? I tried to reason with him; play on his national pride and importance to the team; plead with him; and even demand an extra burst. You can lead a horse to water but you can't make him drink. So I stood in the middle of the Gabba with the ball in my hand, watching him walk away as if he had just done me a favour.

Then in Perth it was on again. I won the toss and put England in to bat, and Hogg had 2–0 as England crashed to 2–3. The visitors were on the run against the seaming new ball on a wicket that gave enormous help to the fast bowlers, and we were in the box seat. So what happens? With dream figures of 2–0 after three overs, Hogg hands me the ball and says he has had enough for the time being and that he is taking a breather. I just stood there in disbelief this time; not able to say a word. You would have to rip a bloke's arm out of the socket to get the ball from him in normal circumstances, but here was Hogg surrendering it – in fact, throwing it away. I copped a fearsome blast of criticism for 'taking him off' and that compounded the situation: he was the one who didn't want to bowl but I was the one who copped the lot from the public and the media.

The most difficult problem I faced was that, despite Hogg's whims, he was bowling magnificently and with extraordinary success. I was more lenient than I would have been but for his success. So I went along to a certain degree with his ideas on field placings, and tried to be philosophical about his short spells. His success with seven wickets in Brisbane, and ten at both Perth and Melbourne, far outweighed the minor problems. I merely adjusted my thinking and counted on him bowling three- or four-over spells, therefore organizing the attack around him. Often that was unfair on Alan Hurst and the other bowlers, but at least I knew Hogg's limit and could figure out a pattern of attack during an innings.

After our great win in Melbourne in the Third Test we were naturally all delighted and looking forward to Sydney. But, once again, relations between Hogg and me went sour. England won the toss and batted, and I was counting on Hogg to wreck the top-order of the batting. But, after a couple of overs, he complained he was having trouble breathing in the exhausting heat and would have to leave the field. At that stage I knew how hot it was and, assuming his asthma was playing up, I felt disappointed but not too upset.

About half an hour later he returned; but it wasn't until later that I discovered that one of the selectors had ordered him back. At the tea interval I went to the doctor and asked how badly Hogg was affected by the asthma, and if he thought I could bowl him after the break without causing him too much difficulty. I was told that Hogg wasn't suffering from asthma, and that as far as the doctor was aware Hogg had not been affected by the ailment for a couple of years. The doctor told me that Hogg was just over-heated earlier in the day by bowling in the heat, and that all he needed was a short rest from the attack to cool down – which I later discovered he could have done on the field.

I was plenty upset about that, and from then on I was sceptical about Hogg's complaints. I kept pardoning him because of his successes during the series, but I realized I had to take a tougher line from then on. After we bowled England out for 169 in Adelaide and managed only 164 ourselves, we needed a fighting effort from our bowlers in the second innings to regain the initiative. We were doing allright, too, when we had England 6–132 in its second innings: with the new ball due early on the third day I felt we could break the Bob Taylor-Geoff Miller partnership and set ourselves up for victory.

That's when the crunch came, early on the third morning of the match. After bowling only four overs to start the day, Hogg walked up to me and said bluntly 'I am going off'. I told him to hang on and asked him why he had to leave the field. He didn't explain and just repeated more forcibly that he was going off. I insisted and he told me to 'get lost' and headed for the pavilion. That was the last straw. Nobody has the right to just walk off the field without explaining to the captain, not to mention asking permission from the umpires. Nobody will ever do that to me again. So I waited and, as time ticked by without Hogg re-emerging from the rooms, I asked the umpires how long he could be off the field without having to wait to bowl once he returned. About midday I asked the umpires if I could leave the field to enquire about Hogg's condition, and they consented. I was running up the pavilion stairs when I saw selector Sam Loxton also heading to the dressing-rooms. I asked the doctor what the trouble was and how long Hogg would be off the field. He told me that Hogg would be right to bowl after lunch after he finished treatment for sore and stiff legs.

That was a relief, because Hogg came back after fifty-four minutes and was able, under the rules, to take the second new ball after the luncheon interval. I was hot under the collar but, at the time, I was more interested in breaking a frustrating and telling partnership. Hogg took the new ball and failed to capture a wicket. He didn't bowl any faster than half pace and did not help the side at all. He let us down badly, and the rest of the players were as upset with his attitude as I was at the time. We were counting on him and he didn't front – not because he wasn't good enough to break the partnership, but because he did not get into top gear at any stage. I blundered because I should have taken him off after two ordinary overs, but I felt that he might shape up and produce as he always has. That he didn't was a crushing blow to us, as Taylor and Miller went on to score a 135-run partnership that eventually won them the Test. To add to the on-field drama at this time, Hogg tried to change the field placings. As I have said, I put up with this to a point because of his success, but now that he had failed to take a wicket and was bowling far below his best, I jumped on him immediately.

This rift had to be sorted out for the benefit of the team and Australian cricket. Unfortunately, I did not have a chance to get him alone that night. The dressing-rooms were the usual hive of activities, and even at a team gathering that night we were surrounded by other players. This was something personal, really, and I wasn't about to have the rest of the team involved. The following day Hogg went to the beach while I travelled to Yallumba for the gala rest day entertainment with most of the other players. So it was left until the morning of the fourth day's play before I could get Hogg alone. I took him aside before play and explained that we had to sort things out.

I told him that I thought there had to be one boss in the side, but that we could work together for the good of the team. He agreed entirely, and said he would pull his weight from then on. The matter was dead and buried as far as I was concerned from that minute on. What is important to say is that this was not a personality clash. I did not go out of my way to make life hard for Hogg, and I am sure he did not try to usurp my authority deliberately. The issues revolved around on-field matters. He has strong opinions on certain aspects of the game and he believes they should be implemented. If I don't agree that they are in the best interests of the team, I say so – and that's when we run headlong into each other. Sorting this out was far easier at this point of the summer because, for the first time, Hogg was not successful. He hadn't claimed a wicket in the second innings and I think that made him realize that cricket is very much a team game and that everybody must pull his weight.

He showed his sincerity when he bowled with all his old fire to capture the last three wickets. The pity was that he had not done so the previous playing day, because we would then have had every chance to win the Test. Nevertheless, the air was cleared and that was one of the major bonuses to come from another disappointing exhibition as we plummeted to a 4–1 series deficit.

The Adelaide Test in fact provided just as much action and drama as any of the series. Even before play began we had several headlines that included the appointment of a liaison officer for the team; a stir about a football coach who gave us a talk on motivation; and Rick Darling's fitness test.

After the hassles of Sydney with the John Maclean injury and an increased workload for me, the suggestion was put forward that the team be given a manager. Kim Hughes really brought the issue to a head when he remarked at a reception in Tasmania that I needed a manager to relieve me of much of the routine and tedious jobs that interfere with my Test match preparation. After I had talks with the chairman of the Australian Cricket Board, Mr Bob Parish, the Board decided to appoint a liaison officer for the Adelaide Test. When the team arrived in Adelaide Les Stillman was there to meet us and he came to our rescue. Les is a former Victorian and South Australian cricketer who is fully aware of the pressures associated with big match preparations and, as he was still playing and a friend or acquaintance of most of the players, he was a magnificent choice. Les organized our practice sessions, cars for our visit, taxis to Government House for a reception, general chores like talking to the press about our activities or whereabouts, and seeing that breakfast orders were in or that everybody was ready to leave for the ground on time. He stayed at the hotel with us and saved me an enormous amount of worry and work about what, on the surface appears to be of minor importance. But when all these incidentals are added to a Test match build-up, the pressures of captaincy, and far more pressing matters like the Rodney Hogg upset, they take on enormous proportions. There was not one off-field mishap in Adelaide, and Les cannot be highly enough recommended for his work in leaving no stone unturned to make every player relaxed and at home.

He helped sort out one item that proved beneficial to the team after a shroud of mystery and media-speculation. Before the season began, Collingwood football coach Tom Hafey addressed the Victorian players and talked about motivation and success. He was a tremendous success and I thought that, in a bid to arouse player enthusiasm, I might try a similar venture with the Australian team.

I didn't necessarily have Hafey in mind : just somebody who was successful in motivating players, regardless of the code, and who would be prepared to talk at our team meeting. Once the idea leaked to the media speculation was rife that either Hafey or North Melbourne's Ron Barassi would be flown to Adelaide for the talk. Naturally that did not win support from the Australian Cricket Board because a lot of money was involved – and in any case that suggestion was not officially put to them. The hullabaloo that followed the initial speculation was amazing. I couldn't say what my plans were because we had not approached anybody; and so I was engaged in a ludicrous press conference where I could not answer questions and the media kept firing them. About mid-afternoon on Test eve we finally had word that South Australian football coach Bob Hammond had accepted our invitation. The Norwood Football Club coach gave us a brief but inspiring chat. That took organization and I was not greatly involved, but the success of the venture was undoubted when we took the field the following day.

Rick Darling proved his fitness after recovering from a cut right hand which he suffered during a charity match at Adelaide Oval a week before. His inclusion was a bonus, as the team already had two new faces in wicketkeeper Kevin Wright and all-rounder Phil Carlson. Wright is a young player of enormous potential, while Carlson was fresh from a dream match for Queensland against New South Wales where he captured ten wickets and scored a century. Although Rick had played only a handful of Tests, he was a key figure in the side, especially after his fine 91 in the first innings of the previous Test. So, relaxed, motivated, and with a full complement, we arrived at Adelaide Oval for the fifth encounter of the summer.

The crowd reacted with a shocked hum when I won the toss and invited Mike Brearley to bat, but this was the greenest Adelaide wicket I had ever seen. Like hell we were going to bat. I much preferred Hogg and Hurst to let loose against them than to have our batsmen subjected to another seaming assault from Mike Hendrick and company. The bowlers rallied behind the decision and spreadeagled the top-order England batsmen.

Alan Hurst started the rout with the prized wicket of Geoff Boycott for 6 in his second over, and an hour later England was tottering at 5–27. Hurst and Hogg were really fired up and they exploited the conditions magnificently. Boycott's dismissal came when the score was 10 with Wright gleefully accepting his first Test scalp as Boycott fended at a rearing delivery. Then Hogg accounted for Brearley with a similarly nasty delivery that sailed through to Wright, and both opening batsmen were out of the way with only 12 runs on the board. Brearley's exit started a collapse in which England lost four wickets for 15 runs in only 33 deliveries. Next to go was Gooch, who suffered a bumper barrage from Hogg during his nervous ten-minute stay. After contributing only one run, he finally gloved a rearing delivery as he took evasive action, and the ball ballooned to Kim Hughes at first slip.

Hurst continued the rout in his opening five overs. He lured Derek Randall into a rash attempt to cover drive, and the thick edge flew like a rocket wide of Phil Carlson at third slip. I thought the ball was on the way to the boundary until Carlson hurled out his right hand and clung to a classic catch as he was still airborne. With Randall out of the way for only 4, Hurst turned his attention to David Gower. The left-hander recorded the first boundary of the innings when he glided a delivery through slips from Hurst, but Hurst had revenge the following delivery.

The ball beat Gower as it speared in sharply from the off-stump before he could jab his bat down. We were jubilant with Gower's dismissal for 9 because that left England 5–27. But we soon lost momentum as Geoff Miller joined Ian Botham. Before he had scored, Miller hooked a delivery from Carlson to Hurst at fine leg, but Hurst made a mess of it. England were 5–35 at the time and the score moved to 5–71 by lunch as the pair enjoyed a 44-run union. Botham and Miller took the score to 80 before Hogg stepped in to comprehensively trap Miller in front of his stumps for 31. That was Hogg's thirty-sixth victim of the series, with which he equalled the fifty-eight-year-old record set by Arthur Mailey as Australia's top wicket-taker in an Ashes campaign. Hogg has improved immensely during the past couple of years and I feel much of his success can be attributed to his magnificent direction. He is always at the batsmen, forcing them to play every delivery. This is most disconcerting for a batsman against a fast bowler with a new ball. He fully deserved his bag of wickets as he thoroughly dominated the opposition throughout the summer with fearsome pace and an unwavering line and length.

We did not have much time to celebrate, however, as Ian Botham decided to attack in the same way that brought him 52 of England's 152 runs in the previous Test first innings. He hopped into Bruce Yardley's off-spin, clouting one delivery over mid-wicket into the members' stand, cutting a boundary and then gliding three more runs through slips from consecutive deliveries. He blasted England past the century – in the brisk time of 160 minutes considering they were six wickets down – and, with solid support from Taylor, he threatened to loosen our grip on proceedings. Fortunately, a spectacular run-out tipped the scales in our favour again. Botham swept a Yardley delivery and Hogg ran thirty metres to cut off what appeared a certain four.

Hogg hurled in a powerful return as Taylor, convinced that there were only three runs in the shot, stood at the batsman's end watching the return. He must have been close to a heart attack as Botham rushed past him while the ball was zooming into Kevin Wright's gloves. Taylor scampered down the wicket, but a cool, underarm throw from Wright to Yardley narrowly caught Taylor out of his ground as he took a spectacular dive for the crease. Botham was the only problem then as England tumbled to 7–113. He hit out lustily with great results, and his cover drives over the fieldsmen were the mark of a fearsome striker of the ball in peak form. He simply slaughtered us, and there was nowhere we could bowl to contain him, or even place a field to stop the run-flow. We simply had to pick up wickets at the other end and try to deprive him of the strike, which was not an easy task as he already had a half-century after only seventy-nine deliveries.

Jim Higgs maintained the pressure when he bowled John Emburey for 4 during his first over as Emburey tried to loft a delivery over mid-wicket. 11 runs later, with the total at 147, Botham lunged forward to a Higgs' delivery and was caught at the wicket for a whirlwind 74, and that should have been it. But Bob Willis had other ideas as he threw his bat at every delivery with astonishing results. He clubbed a cover drive from Hurst for 6 into the members' –

a remarkable sight – and found the middle of the bat for another three boundaries to ruin Hurst's figures. Finally, Hogg returned and, as Willis tried yet another lofted cover drive, Rick Darling charged in to hold a memorable catch. That ended England's innings for 169 after Willis' contribution of 24. What a satisfying sight that scoreboard was. Hogg broke the Mailey record with the wicket of Willis, and he deservedly earned a standing ovation from his home-town crowd and his team-mates.

Hogg captured 4–26 from 10·4 overs and shared the honours with Hurst, who got an important 3–65 including 3–11 in his opening five overs to start the rout, and Jim Higgs who chimed in with 2–9. The trio of Hs could not have been asked for more during this innings and, in fact, they performed magnificently throughout the series. Now all that we needed was a solid start, sensible batting, and our day would be complete.

That dream almost came to a tragic end in the opening over of our innings. Bob Willis charged in and a good length delivery cannoned into Rick Darling's stomach. Rick originally shaped to cut, but the ball cut back so much that he was without protection as it thudded into his body. As the ball came at him he realized he was about to be hit and, instictively, took a deep breath. Suddenly, he collapsed. I thought he was dead as he lay motionless on the ground. There was total silence in the dressing-room and around the ground. When the physiotherapists from the Australian and English camps, the players, and a few other helpers called frantically for a stretcher and started working on Rick's breathing, everybody in the Australian room feared for his life. We were all in a state of shock and extremely concerned about Rick. He had tried so hard to prove his fitness for this Test and is such a good team-man that everyone was upset. Fortunately, word came quickly from the ambulance room that he was all right, but would need a visit to the hospital. Other than a sore and bruised stomach and rib cage, he would be fit. That was the good news, but that still left us wondering what type of hand-grenade Willis was bowling. I watched the replay on television in the players' room, and I was shocked to see the ball seam as viciously as it did at that speed.

Kim Hughes was at an extraordinary disadvantage: he was not aware of Rick's condition when he walked out to join Graeme Wood and play out the last three deliveries of the over. He picked up 4 runs, and was then the victim of a fine, forward diving catch by John Emburey in fourth slip from the bowling of Mike Hendrick. At least I was aware of Rick's condition when I went to the wicket, but the pressure was enormously oppressive. But that was no excuse for picking the wrong line to a Hendrick delivery that cut back and rattled my stumps before I had scored. We were 2–10 with Rick on his way to hospital and with worse to come. Allan Border cracked 11 runs with gusto, but he edged Taylor a catch from the bowling of Ian Botham with the total at 22; and, just two runs later, we lost our fourth wicket when Phil Carlson's first Test innings was a duck. He was adjudged out to the same combination that removed Border. We faced a disastrous collapse.

But Wood and Bruce Yardley, who hit out lustily, took us safely through to stumps, to end a day that turned from a delight to a dissillusioning disappointment. Rick did not require much treatment and, thankfully, he showed enormous courage by declaring he would bat the following day. The medical explanation for his collapse was that he was chewing gum at the time he was hit and, as his tongue curled back, his windpipe was blocked. Once the chewing gum was removed and the windpipe cleared, he breathed normally again and was in no danger. I don't want to see another close call like that again.

Yardley took to the England attack the following morning in the style of Ian Botham. He raced to 28 with a series of cover drives and lofted on-drives before he tried a big hit once too often and was bowled by Botham. His innings was full of merit, because he helped the score to 72 in a 48-run partnership with Wood that quickly wiped off a large slice of our deficit.

Rick Darling then resumed his innings and, with our opening batsmen together again, the new ball gone, and the wicket flattening out, I hoped for a large partnership to regain us the initiative. Rick showed no signs of the previous day's knock and he was putting his body behind the ball and prepared to play his favourite hook. That, unfortun-

95

ately, brought about his downfall. He hooked a Botham delivery to the fence, but could not resist the challenge again, even though England had two men on the boundary in catching positions. He swiped another hook that sailed to Bob Willis at square leg on the fence and was out for 15 with the score at 94. Wood followed with the score at 114 after a fighting innings of 35, in which he played a sheet-anchor role to try to wear out the England bowlers. He was John Emburey's first victim, and then Willis chimed in with Hogg's wicket for a duck. We were back behind the eight-ball at 8–116, still 53 runs in the red. Kevin Wright played a mature innings first-up in Test ranks; and, by driving, hooking, and cutting, he skipped along to 29 as Jim Higgs defended stoutly during a 17-run partnership. Higgs and Hurst then delighted us with an unexpected last wicket partnership of 31 with a strange mixture of Higgs restraint and Hurst aggression. They took our tally to 164 and only a 5-run deficit before Higgs was run out for 16 leaving Hurst unconquered on 17 – a mighty innings for this big Victorian who has no claims as a batsman. Their light-hearted but important partnership virtually made this Test a one-innings match. With less than five sessions gone a result was a definite bet. England had fought back remarkably, and Botham had played as important a role with the ball as he did with the bat, capturing 4–42 from 11·4 overs. Hendrick put us on the road to ruin with two early wickets; he finished with 2–45, while off-spinner Emburey kept up his success rate with 2–13.

England took full advantage of the late afternoon batting strip that had lost its spite, and it eased to 2–82 by stumps. We did not really look like wrecking the top-order, although Phil Carlson captured his first Test scalp, that of Brearley, when he trapped the England skipper in front of his stumps for only 9 with the score on 31. Then Hurst tempted Randall into another indiscreet hook when he was 15, and Bruce Yardley held the chance to make England 2–57. But Geoff Boycott, playing with the stonewall concentration that thwarted us in Perth, carried England through to stumps with the aid of Graham Gooch.

Then the Yallop-Hogg Affair exploded the following morning after Hogg bowled only four overs. That was a

Rodney Hogg
in action

A close call –
Randall and
myself lunge
for the verdict

**Kim Hughes, whose 129 in Brisbane we may never see again

Derek Randall, caught Kim Hughes, bowled Geoff Dymock, in the Benson & Hedges deciding game at the MCG

Graeme Wood loses his stumps for 34, bowled Ian Botham in the Third Test, Melbourne

Champagne after the Third Test win for 'man-of-the-match', Graeme Wood

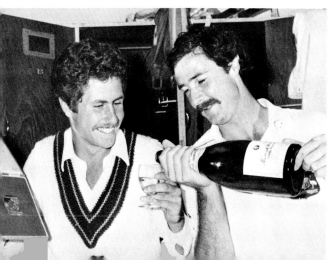

Derek Randall –
a match winner

Jim Higgs during his
marathon 59.6 overs
in the Fourth Test,
Sydney

A friendlier moment between Hogg and myself

A rare sight! Brearley hits out in the final Benson & Hedges Cup Match at the MCG

*The highlight of the summer – victory in the
Benson & Hedges Cup Match competition

Alan Hurst in action

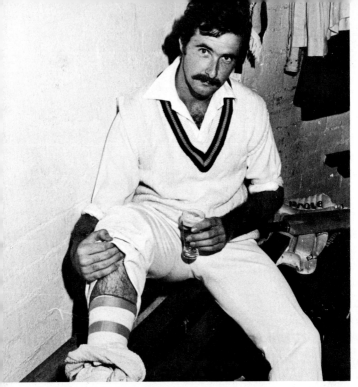

The end of the road for the summer. My calf muscle was torn and I was out of the Second Test against Pakistan

Hogg belts down the stumps in the First Test against Pakistan at the MCG

disappointment, as I have already said. Fortunately, our other bowlers rose to the occasion and stunned the Englishmen by capturing four wickets for 35 runs in only seventy-eight minutes. This was another strange turn of events that began with humble beginnings and developed into a wicket-spree. Carlson started the rot when he squeezed a delivery through a gap between bat and pad and rattled Gooch's stumps for 18 with the total on 95. And then Hurst, bowling with the speed, accuracy, and venom that saved us in the first innings in Sydney, captured the prize wicket of Boycott. Hurst was being frustrated by Boycott who kept coming forward on to the front foot without much worry. So he wound up and let a ripper of a bouncer whiz past the Yorkshireman's nose to really make him stop and think. That was the start of the end for Boycott. A couple of deliveries later he tried to glide a similar delivery through gully and edged a head-high catch to Kim Hughes at first slip. That ended Boycott's four hours and twenty-five minutes innings of 49, and weren't we all delighted. He scored only 10 runs in the opening hour and then took seventeen minutes to move from 48 to 49 before his dismissal. I do not think our spirits could have stayed up in the oppressive heat for too much of the day if he continued in that vein. Hurst kept up the momentum when he accounted for the first innings hero, Botham. Ian, who came in with the score at 4–106, obviously was in murderous form and wanted to take to the attack immediately. He sent a scorching cover drive from Carlson to the fence with ominous power, and I thought that we were in for another taste of his brutal hitting. But he tried a similar shot to Hurst soon after, and this time the ball rocketed off his bat and Bruce Yardley held a magnificent catch. Bruce is not the most solidly-built cricketer in the team and, really, if he hadn't put his hands around the ball, it would have plastered him to the fence.

Gower meanwhile was at his ruthless best. He clouted two boundaries from Hurst and then gave Higgs a minor working-over. But just before lunch he tried to pull a Higgs delivery that kept low and was trapped in front for 21. That left England 6–132 and with a lead of only 137. With all the recognized batsmen back in the pavilion, we were again in control. With the second new ball awaiting us shortly after lunch I felt that we could go on with the rout and face only a minor second innings target.

Taylor and Miller had other ideas. They came out fighting after the interval, and clubbed 28 runs from five overs, with Miller hooking Hurst to the fence twice and Taylor gliding, pushing, and nudging runs with great success. I took the new ball with the score at 161 but, with Hogg bowling below his best and Hurst wilting under the strain of so much early morning work, we failed to break through. The bowlers and fieldsmen were showing obvious effects from the heat and, before we knew it, the new ball had come and gone and Taylor and Miller had a half-century stand in only seventy minutes. Miller took full toll of the situation and he played several fine drives and sweeps, while Taylor actually surprised me with a couple of sweetly-timed drives to accompany his dabs. The runs just kept coming, the pair became completely at home, and suddenly a century partnership was on the board in the brisk time of 160 minutes.

The lion-hearted Hurst finally ended the union when he found the edge of Miller's bat as the batsman attempted a glance. Wright held the low chance and England was 7–267. That was just eleven minutes before stumps. The partnership had yielded 135 runs in 231 minutes to come within eight runs of the record seventh-wicket partnership created by Frank Woolley and Joe Vine in 1911-12. By stumps England was 7–272 and had us under the hammer again, with Taylor unbeaten on 69. His previous highest Test score was 45 and the way he was batting assured us that he had a few more gems up his sleeve for the fourth day's play. I fancy Miller is a useful player but I do not think he is top class as an all-rounder. But he certainly did his job competently this day, as did Taylor, who showed what concentration and dedication are all about, even if you haven't a large array of shots.

We all needed the rest day. The weather had been over-bearing for several weeks, really, and I think it was taking a toll. I know that Hurst must have appreciated it. He bowled seventeen overs during the third day for figures of 3–48 in a marathon performance, and there was more to come.

Taylor and John Emburey carried England past 300 as we toiled in the field for more than ten hours in this second innings, and they posted a half-century partnership in eighty-one minutes. We were now axiously waiting for the third new ball of the innings as Bruce Yardley conceded 25 runs from four overs. Finally it came ... and was just about gone again after six overs. Then Taylor, who had shown enormous concentration in the heat for such a long time, edged the last ball of Hogg's fourth over to Wright down the leg side in the final over before lunch. Taylor's innings of 97 was a superb innings, really, because I never rated him a player capable of more than 30 or so. But he plugged away, played a series of drives, persisted with his dabs here and there and, in the end, was deserving of a century. He thwarted us for almost five and a half hours, hit six 4s, and helped the score from 132 to 336 before he departed. It was truly a courageous and telling exhibition.

Hogg, with his first success of the innings behind him, then wrapped up the innings. He uprooted Emburey's off-stump with a blistering delivery, after the English spinner had added 42 runs in two and a half hours. Again, it was the England tail that had halted us, and this time it was a most important hurdle of runs and time. Hogg then had Willis caught at the wicket for 12 to end the innings at 360. Hogg captured 3-16 on this fourth day to finish the innings with 3-59 from 27·6 overs. But the innings honours went to Hurst, who bowled a marathon effort of thirty-seven overs for 4-97. England left us 366 runs for victory in 550 minutes and, although the contract was not easy, the wicket was now good enough to give us heart for the challenge.

By stumps on the fourth day we were 2-82 after losing Rick Darling and Graeme Wood. The pair added 31 before Rick stepped inside a Botham delivery and lost his leg-stump for 18; and five runs later, Wood was run out in amazing circumstances. Graeme, who picked up the nickname of 'Kamikaze Kid' because of his running between wickets, was downright unlucky this time. He hit a delivery from Botham to Boycott at mid-on and headed off for a sharp single. Boycott picked up the ball and threw down the stumps with Graeme out of his ground.

But he was out of his ground only because Botham had

backed into him, forced him to run via the Black Stump and then almost collect the umpire who was running across his path. I was furious, especially after I watched the replay on the dressing-room television set before I went into bat. Graeme may have been out of his ground, but morally he should not have been given out. I am not saying that Botham deliberately baulked Wood, but he certainly interfered with his attempt to complete his run. As it turned out umpire Bailhache did not take any notice of Graeme's plea about the interference, and umpire O'Connell either was not looking at that end or also felt that it was 'just one of those things'.

Graeme was naturally most upset, but the damage was done. He was back in the pavilion for only 9 after just more than an hour's batting, and Kim Hughes and I had to see Australia safely through the few minutes before tea and onwards to stumps. We did that without too much trouble although we concentrated mainly on protecting our wickets. After the Sydney collapse, I wanted to ensure we were there to start the final day and not allow the England bowlers to dictate terms. We did not win much credit for our tactics with only 46 runs in 130 minutes together, but that did not worry us. Had we gone silly and attempted to belt the England bowlers at that stage – and lost wickets as we did in Sydney – we could have been bagged. We had a little laugh that night because we realized we could not win with some critics no matter how we played the game.

I was not laughing by mid-afternoon the next day when we were skittled for a paltry 160 to lose the Test and trail 4–1 in the series.

Kim and I decided to play our natural game when play resumed as the wicket was in good condition, the sun was shining, and the ball was forty overs old. With a target of 284 in five hours and fifteen overs in the final hour, we felt that a win was not out of the realms of possibility. So we determined from the start to treat each delivery on its merits and see how the game unfolded. Kim and I were confronted by Emburey and Miller at the start and, as they had close-in fieldsmen, we lofted deliveries into the vacant outfield, stole singles, and upset the England attack no-end. We rattled past the 100. At this stage Mike Brearley had to

100

take both bowlers out of the firing line. That was not a genius move, although he was given credit for such, because Kim and I had pasted his bowlers all over the field and he had no option.

But what followed made him look as if he had calculated the introduction of Mike Hendrick and Bob Willis. Nothing could be further from the truth. He had to bring both bowlers into action to try to stem the run-flow, and I am sure he did not want to introduce them at that stage because the new ball was due in some fifteen overs time and would have been a better bet for this pair. Anyway, Hendrick started a collapse that ended in another dismal display. We lost eight wickets for 45 runs in little more than an hour and a half. I was the first to go with the score on 115, after Kim and I added 79 runs in 178 minutes, including 33 in forty-eight minutes on that final morning. I once again played the wrong line to a delivery from Hendrick, and edged the ball on to my stumps after scoring 36. Hendrick then claimed Kim's wicket for a fine innings of 46, when a cover drive screwed off his bat towards Gower where this acrobatic fieldsman had an extraordinary diving catch. Hendrick had 2–0 in ten deliveries, and then Willis really nailed us to the wall. He bowled Allan Border for 1 and, two deliveries later, had Bruce Yardley caught in first slip by Brearley for a duck while Bruce was attempting a rather breezy cover-drive. Willis then had 2–0 and we were on skid row at 6–121.

Miller then returned for the mopping-up operation. He gave Emburey an easy bat-pad catch from Wright's defensive bat before our wicketkeeper had scored, and then he bowled Hogg for a duck. So we were 8–130 and shot to bits. In just one hour we had lost 6–15, the Test, hopes of squaring the series, regaining lost honour from Sydney, and all confidence. Carlson hit out for 21 and Hurst for 13, but the result was a formality. The end came with the score on 160, giving England a comprehensive victory by 205 runs. The last time an Australian team was down 4–1 in a series was in the 1932–3 Bodyline series, and no Australian cares to remember that. I did not want to think too much about this exhibition either. I felt we had the nucleus of a good side: our bowlers were penetrating; we had the benefit of choosing what we could do with four toss-wins in five Tests; and, as individuals, our batsmen had shown promise and form. We simply had to put it together, stop these inexcusable collapses, and show more endeavour and commonsense.

That is not taking credit away from the Englishmen. Mike Hendrick bowled magnificently in this innings – as he did all summer – and Bob Willis returned to the fiery bowler that wrecked us in the opening two Tests with thirteen wickets. He captured 3–41 in our second innings, while Hendrick took the honours with 3–19 from fourteen overs. They didn't have much more going for them than we did with the ball but, while our batsmen succumbed, the Englishmen showed a lot more grit. We had to learn from Bob Taylor and Geoff Miller. Simply, we had to learn and show on the field what we had gained from the experience.

8   One-day Stand

How sweet it is. After a hiding in the series, loss of the Ashes by a record margin, and a stream of abuse from all and sundry, Australia finally showed its mettle with a totally unexpected victory in the one-day competition Gold Cup. This was the moment I had been waiting for as I stood at the MCG accepting the magnificent Cup after coming from a first match thrashing to steal the second round and then annihilate England in the deciding match. At last we showed we could learn by our mistakes, even against a team that is renowned for its prowess in the one-day style of cricket.

The one-day competition suffered greatly because of rain during the series, with washouts in Melbourne and then Sydney; but, by re-scheduling the itinerary, the Board managed to organize the three days for the competition. As I said, there was not much left to achieve after the Adelaide Test apart from a large slice of prestige and, even before we hit Melbourne for the remaining two one-day games in early February, we were behind the eight-ball.

Before the Adelaide Test we were comprehensively beaten by England in the first one-day encounter. They took us apart, really, showing up our naïvety in this type of cricket, and coasting to a walkover win of seven wickets. After we batted first and managed only 101 in 33·5 overs, England had no difficulty in pacing itself to score 3–102. We started on the right foot, but then our batsmen tried to hit over the top of the fieldsmen and holed out. We began to collapse and that was it. The innings lasted only 197 minutes and, from 1–27, we were skittled for another 74 with 11 extras in our total. England was never really under pressure in its chase. Boycott squeezed singles and took 28·2 overs to accumulate 39 runs, while the other batsmen played a few more daring shots. As a result they cruised to the total in 153 minutes with 11·6 overs of the 40 allotted to spare. That was a real hammering, no matter which way you look at it.

The word was out that we would take an even bigger pummelling in the World Cup in June in England if that sort of performance continued. So, after that drubbing, the Adelaide loss, and pessimistic outlooks all round, we arrived in Melbourne for the next two one-day matches. If all of this wasn't enough, we also had a few pre-match upsets. Hogg was still sore and could not play in the matches, and then came another bombshell – Rick Darling was dropped from the following Test team for Sydney.

That news caused horror-waves around Australia in the media, because Rick was not told of his dismissal until he reached Melbourne for the one-day game and was met at the airport by the press. I did not know about it until I heard it on the radio, and I must say I was surprised. So, besides the pressures of having to pull our socks up on the field in the coming matches, we also had a situation where Rick was in the team for the one-day games and out for the next Test. That upset our harmony a little, even before a delivery was bowled two days later. Everybody felt sorry for Rick, who tried so hard to pass a fitness test to play in Adelaide, only to be felled by Willis. Then he suffered the shock of this news. The media immediately criticized the Board for not telling Darling while he was in Adelaide or at least before he heard it from them hours and hours after the team announcement. I think that this sort of situation is not good for the relationships between the players and the Board. Something must be done to avoid it in future. The selectors chose the team the previous night in Adelaide on the final day of the match, and it was announced about lunchtime the following day, the Friday. Rick caught a plane from Adelaide to Melbourne on Friday morning – so that gave the selectors about eighteen hours to pull him aside and tell him. That could have been done quietly so that the team announcement was not pre-empted, while at the same time saving the player all the embarrassment and hostility of hearing it from the media, the airport attendant, or the taxi driver. Relations between the players and the Board have improved enormously in recent years in many areas and are still improving in leaps and bounds. This is one area, however, that could be improved for the sake of the player, team harmony, and the public image of the

Board. Rick copped it sweet on the surface, but the damning criticism that the media gave the Board did not help the Board's public image.

I saw Rick in the rooms on the Sunday morning of the next match and, like everyone else, gave him my sympathy. What more could you say? He knew he had to fight back by performing on the field and he accepted that, which helped cheer us up no-end. The selectors were right on the ball with this team for the one-day game, as it had to boast a largely different type of cricketer than in Tests. With Hogg out, Geoff Dymock came in, while hard hitting all-rounders Gary Cosier and Trevor Loughlin came in for spinners Bruce Yardley and Jim Higgs.

The second match of the series was of enormous importance to us. A loss would end all hopes of winning anything during the summer, and we would merely add weight to the knockers' arguments. We had to do well, show we had learned from the initial one-day hiding, and keep alive our hopes of winning the Cup.

I won the toss and put England in to bat. We were off to a marvellous start when Dymock had Boycott (0) and Randall (4) back in the pavilion with only 7 runs on the board. Then England steadied with Brearley and Gooch adding 43 in an hour, before Gooch holed out off Carlson for 19. That brought David Gower to the wicket, and he absolutely slaughtered us. With help from Brearley (33) and later Ian Botham (31 in forty-six minutes), he cut and pulled and hooked and swept and drove to all parts of the field. You just could not bowl to the man. We tried to bowl outside off-stump and he pounded the ball over covers or jumped inside it and pulled. We attacked his stumps and he just hit it where he fancied. Chris Old joined him after Botham and then David Bairstow – the wicketkeeper who flew to Australia to join the party after Roger Tolchard was injured in Newcastle earlier on tour – left the fray with the total at 6–158, and he and Gower hit to their hearts' content. As the overs ran out England scooted past 200 and, with just one delivery to play, Gower had the strike with his score on 97. I put a ring of fieldsmen most of the way back to the fence as Laughlin came in to bowl. I did not want them too far back, because he might have been

105

able to scamper through for three runs for his century, and I felt that if he could hit the ball over or through the fieldsmen for four he deserved the 'ton' anyway. Laughlin bowled and Gower jumped down the wicket, hitting it on the up with such power that the five guys on the off-side boundary had no chance whatsoever to cut it off as it raced along the ground.

That was absolutely brilliant. He deserved a century, and what a superb innings it was – just 100 deliveries for 101 runs in a total of 6–212. His driving was a delight. The shots just flowed, and I have not seen anything like it for years. He justly won the man-of-the-match award later.

Well, that was all well and good, but didn't we have a mountain of a target? We had to start well and build our innings methodically. I was not interested in how many runs we required per over. All we had to do was keep up with them or as close to them as possible and sum up the situation – hopefully with plenty of wickets in hand – with about ten overs to go. Rick and Graeme Wood were together for only 7 runs before Rick cut a ball from Willis to Old at backward point, but then we settled down. Wood and Kim Hughes added 42 runs for the second wicket before Wood was bowled trying to lash out at a delivery from Old when 23. Kim and I then took the score to 90 when Kim was out for a fine innings of 50, which included four boundaries, to consolidate our innings and keep us in touch with the scoring-rate. Peter Toohey then joined me. We had to steady the innings at this stage lest we collapsed, and we decided to steal singles here and there and give any loose deliveries a real nudge. The ploy was successful, and we took the tally to 145. With ten of the allotted forty overs remaining our score was 3–125, and we required 88 to win. That was right on the cards and, suddenly, the Englishmen began to feel the pinch for one of the few occasions during the summer. The bowlers and fieldsmen had a few words and even Mike Brearley copped an occasional backhanded comment. Toohey and I hammered 9 runs from the first of the final ten overs, and then ran 4 to start the next. But then I was out for 31 with the score at 145, leaving us 68 runs to win with eight overs remaining. As I walked off the ground Gary Cosier came down the race and said 'Are we still going for them?' I just smiled at him in a wry way, and he said 'You beauty, it's slogging time.' Indeed it was.

He clubbed 28 runs in twenty-four minutes from only fourteen deliveries. Two of his shots were lofted drives to the fence, and then he hit a tremendous straight six into the members' that cleared the fence by a long, long way. Watching from the players' room we lost the ball, because it went about fifty metres into the air on its path to the terrace seats. That broke the back of the struggle, even though Gary was bowled by John Lever with the total at 185 and Phil Carlson also went at that score before he contributed a run.

But we had plenty of big hitters. Trevor Laughlin went in to accompany Toohey, and he thumped a six and a boundary to be 15 not out in twenty-one minutes. Peter Toohey was unbeaten on 54 in a fine innings as we moved to victory with ten deliveries to spare. The victory was an enormous shock to the Englishmen, who felt sure we would collapse as we did in the Tests and in the earlier one-day game. Against all the odds, when they thought they were set up with a score of 212 and a string of experienced, professional one-day specialist bowlers, we bounced back to skittle them. The feeling in the rooms was electric – just like at the end of a grand final football win. Players and officials cheered and drank champagne, and we knew we had proved a point in the most difficult circumstances. All we needed then was to go on and win the following match two days later to take out the Cup and we could hold our heads high as one-day champions.

And one-day champions we were. We completely turned the tables on the Englishmen in this game. They annihilated us the first game, we stole the second game from them, and in the decider we whipped them unmercifully. Looking back, this was the most satisfying part of the summer. The turnabout was most impressive, and we suddenly loomed as a threat in any one-day competition, especially the coming World Cup. We knew after this Cup win that we did have the talent, and that we were capable of producing it whether chasing a big score or by bowling the opposition out and crushing them.

The third match once again started with Geoff Dymock

making early inroads. He dismissed Boycott for 1, and then Randall for a duck, and was on a hat-trick as England tottered at 2–10 after only four overs. Then Hurst stepped in, claiming the scalps of Gooch for 4 and Gower for 3.

Gower's dismissal was the major break we needed. We noticed during his century innings on the Sunday – and in fact during the entire summer – that he tends to cut deliveries on the up, and hit them hard but in the air through backward-point. So I put Toohey there immediately, and Gower hit a cut just wide of him before he had scored. But the following over he hammered a delivery from Hurst directly to Wood in that position and fell for the trap. Brearley and Botham held us up temporarily for 20 runs, before Botham tried to hit a delivery from Cosier out of the ground and played it on to his stumps. England was 5–42 and soon after 6–56 as Bairstow was run out for 3. Really, we did not have too much to worry about after that, although Brearley and Phil Edmonds added 35 runs for the next wicket. Edmonds wasn't too impressed with wide-of-the-stump bowling by Laughlin, an at one stage he uprooted his leg-stump and repositioned it wide of the crease on the off-side. It was rather amusing, really, because three balls later Laughlin trapped him in front of his stumps for 15. Brearley then went for 46 as England lost its last four wickets for three runs, to be all out for 94.

They had lasted only 31·7 overs and 166 minutes. From our point of view that more than compensated for our first match batting failure. All we had to do was bat sensibly, wipe off the runs, and clinch that $11,500 Gold Cup and the championship.

The lads were rather toey, I might tell you, and Wood and Darling batted as if there was no tomorrow. They clobbered 29 runs from the opening thirty-eight deliveries to settle the issue. We lost Rick for 14 as he hit a Willis slower ball to Brearley in the covers, and then Kim Hughes fell for the same trap before he had scored. Wood and I took us past the half-way mark and on to 54 before Wood was caught at the wicket from Botham for 30, and I was a victim of that infamous 87 after scoring 25 and trying to belt John Lever out of the ground. That left Toohey and Cosier to wrap it up, and secure a six-wicket victory.

Standing on the dais accepting the trophy in front of the MCG crowd was a moment I will cherish. The boys really fought hard for this. I think we proved to ourselves, the public, and the opposition that we were building a spirit and combination that had a future at the top.

BENSON & HEDGES CUP
MATCH ONE, MELBOURNE, 23 JANUARY
Toss: **Australia**

AUSTRALIA

G. Wood c Gower b Edmonds	28
A. Hilditch c Bairstow b Botham	10
A. Border c Willis b Hendrick	11
K. Hughes l.b.w. Hendrick	0
G. Yallop run out	9
P. Carlson c Randall b Willis	11
T. Laughlin c Willis b Hendrick	6
J. Maclean c Edmonds b Botham	11
R. Hogg c Botham b Hendrick	4
G. Dymock c & b Botham	1
A. Hurst not out	0
Extras	10
Total	101

Fall: 27, 52, 54, 55, 76, 78, 94, 99, 101, 101

Bowling: R. Willis 8–4–15–1, J. Lever 5–2–7–0, M. Hendrick 8–1–25–4, I. Botham 4·5–2–16–3, P. Edmonds 7–0–26–1, G. Gooch 1–0–2–0
Innings time: 197 minutes. Overs: 33·5

ENGLAND

G. Boycott not out	39
M. Brearley b Hogg	0
D. Randall c Yallop b Dymock	12
G. Gooch b Carlson	23
D. Gower not out	19
Extras	9
Three wickets for	102

Fall: 7, 29, 69

Bowling: R. Hogg 6–1–20–1, G. Dymock 6–1–16·1, T. Laughlin 5–1–13–0, P. Carlson 5–0–21–0, A. Hurst 5·2–1–14–0, A. Border 1–0–9–0
Innings time: 153 minutes. Overs: 28·2
England won by seven wickets
Man-of-the-match: M. Hendrick (England)

Toss: Australia

ENGLAND

M. Brearley c Wright b Dymock	0
G. Boycott l.b.w. Laughlin	33
D. Randall l.b.w. Dymock	4
G. Gooch c Hurst b Carlson	19
D. Gower not out	101
I. Botham c Wood b Hurst	31
D. Bairstow run out	1
C. Old not out	16
Extras	7
Six wickets for	212

Fall: 0, 7, 50, 89, 153, 158

Bowling: A. Hurst 8–1–36–1, G. Dymock 8–1–31–2, P. Carlson 8–1–27–1, G. Cosier 8–0–48–0, T. Laughlin 8–0–63–1

Innings time: 200 minutes. Overs: 40

AUSTRALIA

R. Darling c Old b Willis	7
G. Wood b Old	23
K. Hughes c Boycott b Lever	50
G. Yallop c Gower b Hendrick	31
P. Toohey not out	54
G. Cosier b Lever	28
P. Carlson c Brearley b Lever	0
T. Laughlin not out	15
Extras	7
Six wickets for	215

Fall: 7, 55, 90, 145, 185, 185

Bowling: R. Willis 8–1–21–1, C. Old 8–1–31–1, M. Hendrick 8–0–47–1, J. Lever 7–1–51–3, I. Botham 7·6–0–58–0

Innings time: 230 minutes. Overs: 38·6

Australia won by four wickets

Man-of-the-match: D. Gower (England)

BENSON & HEDGES CUP
MATCH THREE, MELBOURNE, 7 FEBRUARY
Toss: Australia

ENGLAND

G. Boycott c Cosier b Dymock	2
M. Brearley c Wright b Cosier	46
D. Randall c Hughes b Dymock	0
G. Gooch c Hughes b Hurst	4
D. Gower c Wood b Hurst	3
I. Botham b Cosier	13
D. Bairstow run out	3
P. Edmonds l.b.w. Laughlin	15
J. Lever b Laughlin	1
R. Willis c Wright b Cosier	2
M. Hendrick not out	0
Extras	5
Total	94

Fall: 10, 10, 17, 22, 42, 56, 91, 91, 94, 94

Bowling: A. Hurst 5–3–22–3, G. Dymock 6–1–21–2, P. Carlson 8–2–22–0, G. Cosier 7–1–22–3, T. Laughlin 5·7–0–17–2
Innings time: 166 minutes. Overs: 31·7

AUSTRALIA

G. Wood c Bairstow b Botham	30
R. Darling c Brearley b Willis	14
K. Hughes c Brearley b Willis	0
G. Yallop b Lever	25
P. Toohey not out	16
G. Cosier not out	8
Extras	2
Four wickets for	95

Fall: 29, 37, 54, 87

Bowling: R. Willis 5–2–16–2, M. Hendrick 6–0–32–0, I. Botham 5·5–0–30–1, J. Lever 5–0–15–1
Innings time: 127 minutes. Overs: 21·5
Australia won by six wickets
Man-of-the-match: G. Dymock (Australia)

9   Ashes to Ashes

The euphoria that surrounded our one-day Cup victory
was crushed in no uncertain terms when we played the final
Test in Sydney. We were given another drubbing, this time
by nine wickets, as we batted badly on a magnificent bat-
ting-strip on the first day, and then collapsed against the
England spinners as the wicket turned into a 'minefield'.
The victory gave England a 5–1 series win, a most lopsided
result. But I do not believe that there was as much
difference between the teams as indicated in the 5–1 figures,
although England's experience, all-rounders, and profes-
sionalism certainly kept them just that much ahead throughout. When I look back and think that we had an attack of
Rodney Hogg with forty-one record-breaking wickets, Alan
Hurst with twenty-three scalps, four century-makers, the
benefit of five toss victories to one, and still took that hiding, I just can't believe the overall result.

We had England down so many times in the series without being able to ram home the advantage that it was totally
frustrating. That was partly due to their never-say-die spirit,
experience and talent, and largely due to our own inex-
perience. Luck flowed their way regularly, while we copped
the rough end of the deal, overall, with vital umpiring decisions. And, of course, they had the benefit of wickets that
suited them and which were basically alien to us – seaming
strips in Brisbane and Perth, and spinner's strips in Sydney
on both occasions. England skipper Mike Brearley went
to lengths to express this imbalance in the overall result,
and said that Australia boasted plenty of talent and could
be a strength in the near future. I know that to be true.
Once our players learn to put all the ingredients together –
as we did in Melbourne's Third Test – we will enjoy far
greater success. There was a result in every match. That
should not have been the case, really: we could have
drawn in Brisbane and Perth, and won in the Fourth Test
in Sydney and the Fifth in Adelaide. Our batsmen let us
down badly throughout the series. When one of our bats-

men was in form and on top, the rest did not support him, but surrendered their wickets too easily. The Englishmen made us fight every inch of the way for their wickets and it was a credit to our bowlers that they constantly routed them. On the other hand, our batsmen made it easy for England with inexcusable run outs and indiscreet shots.

On so many occasions during the series I felt we were starting to put it together, only to see us squander winning chances that allowed England back into the game or even to take complete control, which is a facet of play that has to be eliminated. Nobody can deny the talent at our disposal in the batting department, I just don't think that the players have enough confidence in themselves to produce their best consistently. So much of the talent remains basically untapped, springing to the surface maybe only one innings in three or four. That is not good enough in Test ranks, and can only be corrected by experience and determined effort.

I felt we worked out the Englishmen fairly well and kept them under pressure when batting almost throughout the entire series. They sorted out a few of our batsmen too, but the players did not have the know-how or determination to alter their game or technique to force a new approach from the opposition. This meant that a few players were falling for the same trap, making life easy for the opposition bowlers. Those that did work it out had success. They will have a lot more in the near future.

I felt the difference between the two teams in terms of an individual was Mike Hendrick. He was by far the best bowler in the England team, always at the batsmen with pace and movement, and capable of coming on to bowl on a spot for over after over. He wrecked us on several occasions, although he did not return the figures. But the man I would have liked even more in the Australian side was Ian Botham. We were short of an all-rounder who could take an attack by the scruff of the neck and swing a game, and who could also open with the new ball and field in any position with brilliance. With Botham in our side for the summer I fancy the series could have resulted in our favour.

The man of the series was, no doubt, Rodney Hogg for Australia. He captured a record-breaking forty-one wickets at an average of 12·85 in a superb exhibition. He had the better of every English batsman, and I hope he improves even more and plays for Australia for a long time to come. In terms of wickets and striking power he left the other bowlers for dead, and he repeatedly gave us every chance to get on the road to victory.

When we arrived in Sydney for this Sixth and final Ashes Test we were full of confidence. Admittedly, there is a major difference between one-day games and a Test match, but we had shown that we could topple England if we approached the game sensibly. Out of the victorious one-day team went Cosier, Laughlin, Darling and Dymock, while Andrew Hilditch came in for his Test debut; Hogg returned, and so did spinners Bruce Yardley and Jimmy Higgs.

We were immediately off on the wrong foot. The practice wickets at the Sydney Cricket Ground this summer have been extremely poor, and training was virtually impossible. After the John Maclean injury in the Fourth Test I don't think many of the lads had much confidence in the wickets on the Number 2 Oval, and training was basically restricted to the centre wicket of that ground, and fielding. This was not really good enough, and it was impossible on the eve of the Test with both the Australian and English teams there at the same time. We arrived first and took over the centre wicket for an hour, and then allowed the visitors a chance. But throughout the session cricket balls were flying in all directions as some players used the nets and hit into the centre of the ground, batsmen in the center wicket cut into the net area behind them, and fieldsmen swamped the ground. Mike Brearley was not very impressed, and neither was I. We were trying to prepare for a Test that was important for both sides and, really, that was a farcical training session for both camps.

I was also on the end of another blast from the Sydney media, who seemed to take delight at getting my name into their papers whenever anything went wrong. Two days before the Test the team arrived in Sydney and scheduled practice for later that afternoon. I had to pick up a car to use during my stay and, on the way to the ground, the car broke down. I was stranded for an hour, and arrived at the training an hour late. Anybody would have thought I had abandoned the team for a session during the Test. I was hot, irritable, and frustrated, and I rushed into the rooms to get changed into my gear to join the training. I might say that I was not impressed with Jim Woodward of the Sydney *Telegraph* who yelled to me from the bar area wanting an explanation. Later he saw me on the field, and I told him I was 'on business' because I hadn't cooled down from the earlier dramas.

That was big news the following day as I was branded a villain – yet again. As I have said earlier, I did not think much of some of the media treatment of the Australian team, and myself particularly, during the summer. This, particularly, was a case of blowing a story out of all proportions. I wasn't getting on too well with Woodward and a few other newspapermen at that stage, and I think it all caught up with me when Woodward shouted to me from the bar. I don't class that as a press conference, and I gave him a curt answer. I could easily have explained my whereabouts to Jim had he approached me at an appropriate time and in an appropriate place, and had I given him the story as it happened there no doubt would not have been the sensational article in the papers the following day.

I have to sharpen up on my thoughts about the media perhaps, or perhaps a few media men should think more about the game and stop trying to grab headlines with petty stories at every opportunity. The Sydney press were notorious on occasions. Dick Tucker of the *Mirror* and Norman Tasker of the *Sun* gave us an awful caning, time and again, calling for the axe for everybody but the boot-strapper on a couple of occasions – and then offering no alternatives as replacements. All right, we put in some very poor performances at times. But, instead of making constructive criticism, they wanted us out, one and all. If it wasn't so damaging and annoying to the team, it could have been funny at times comparing the Sydney papers: how many have you thrown out today and how nasty can your headline get? Maybe there was a competition going, because the Sydneysiders seemed to adopt the motto 'If you can't say something nasty about them, don't say anything at all'. Like the one-day Cup match that was scheduled for two days after the Fourth Test: I cannot recall seeing one paragraph in the afternoon papers about that game on the eve of the match. If you lived in Sydney you would have been lucky to know it was on.

Having said that, I had a word after training to a group of pressmen on the eve of the final Test – two of the four Sydney pressmen weren't there, unfortunately, because they didn't attend the training – and I tried to sort out a few problems about our relationship.

I think that talk did a lot of good, and I only wish some of the men there had been forward enough to talk as straight as they did at the start of the season as at that time. A couple of the pressmen who toured around Australia hadn't even had a drink with me, a friendly chat, or meal. The only time I saw many of them was at the end-of-day press conference. Maybe they thought I was stand-offish, but that was not the case. I was available on many occasions. All it needed was a phone call, or even a word in the dressing-rooms after a day's play to organize a beer and a chat. The press stayed with the English touring team during the series. That is fair enough, as they have to tour with them for three months or so while the Australians gather for only four or five weeks outside the pressman's home city. But we were never far away.

That sorted out, I concentrated on the Test. The SCG wicket was, as it had been during the Fourth Test, a marvellous batting wicket on the first morning, which would obviously crumble later. I won my fifth toss in six Tests and jumped at the chance to bat. Oh dear, did we foul this up.

Graeme Wood and his new partner Andy Hilditch put 18 runs on the board in even time and everything looked rosy. And then, as it happened with frustrating monotony this series, we lost our first wicket by virtue of an inexcusable run out. Andy glided a delivery from Mike Hendrick into the gully and started to charge down the wicket, unaware that Graham Gooch had the ball covered as he dived from slip. Gooch returned the ball to the stumps as Andy came to a grinding halt in the middle of the wicket. He realized that Wood was not coming towards him, but just failed to regain his ground. It was another wasted wicket that the tourists hadn't had to work for to any degree. Then Hendrick moved a delivery off the seam and found the defensive edge of Wood's bat, and Ian Botham held a super catch as he hurled himself to his right from second slip as the ball headed for the turf in front of his skipper. Wood was out for 15. I joined Kim Hughes with the score 2–19 after only half an hour.

Kim and I decided to defend grimly for the time being to see out the new-ball attack of Willis and Hendrick. But, once Ian Botham came into the fray, I decided it was time to start the scoreboard ticking over again. I took 12 runs from his first over with a trio of cuts to the boundary and then, as spinner Embury came into the bowling line up, Kim swept him to the fence to move from 2 after three-quarters of an hour. My assault on Botham resulted in 20 runs from four overs and Brearley had to replace him with Hendrick. That proved a bonus for England, as Hendrick captured Hughes' wicket with the opening delivery of the last over before lunch. Kim presented Botham with another second slip catch after sticking at the crease for 101 minutes for 16. That left us 3–67 at the first change, and in a disappointing position despite a 48-run partnership in brisk time between Kim and me.

Peter Toohey contributed only 8 runs after lunch as he tried to hold up an end during a 34-run partnership in forty-seven minutes. But he fell victim to Botham when he edged Taylor a catch at the wicket, and we were in trouble at 4–101. Phil Carlson then couldn't handle a Botham bouncer, and he gloved a catch to Gooch in the gully after only 2 runs. With the score at 5–109 I had no option but to have a lash in a bid to build respectability into the innings. I really enjoyed hitting Willis and Botham, and I was in my best form of the year against the spinners, hitting them over the top of mid-wicket at every chance. That is my pet shot against the spinners. I don't actually hit across the line of the ball, because I get down the wicket and position myself to aim and swing in that direction. If I miss the ball hits me on the pads well down the track this day I wasn't missing many as I found plenty of time to pick up the flight and hit into the open spaces. While was having a feast the rest of the boys were struggling. Bruce Yardley was bowled by Emburey for 7 and Kevin Wright was stumped as he charged down the wicket when 3. We were 7–124. With only Hogg, Higgs, and Hurst to follow I knew an all-out assault was the only chance. Botham came back, and I gave him everything I had. He attacked my leg-stump, and I swung him over leg time and again while Brearley tried to plug the on-side. I just couldn't believe it. It is mighty difficult stopping runs when you bowl on the leg stump, especially to a left-hander, and try to set your field to suit. I thought Brearley would have been far wiser bowling outside off-stump and stacking the covers. But I wasn't complaining as I headed towards a century.

Hogg stuck around for forty-five minutes in a valuable innings and, although he scored only 9 runs, he shared in a partnership of 35. Then Jimmy Higgs walked in and told me to have a go and he would keep up his end – which he did marvellously for fifty-two minutes. In that time we added 39 runs to reach 198. I passed my century in that time and went on to score 121 before I was out trying another big hit from the bowling of Botham. Hurst failed to score and that was our lot; a dismal 198 on a perfect batting wicket. My innings took 266 minutes and included thirteen boundaries. The other ten batsmen could manage only 72 runs between them, with another five extras. The lack of support was bitterly disappointing. Yet again there was no solidarity, and this time there were no excuses – the wicket was perfect and the weather ideal for batting. Wood (15) and Hughes (16) were the only others to reach double figures, but the men who showed how easy it really was were Hogg and Higgs. They just played down the line and defended stoutly and let the runs come. We were in real trouble, and I realized at the end of our innings that only a miracle could get us back into the game. The Englishmen had all the time in the world and, naturally, they played accordingly.

Hurst made our first inroad into the England line-up when he had Boycott caught at slip by Hilditch for 19 after an hour and a half with the total on 37. Boycott was reluctant to leave the scene, pointing to the ground in front of Hilditch at second slip. I had a clear view of the catch from mid-on, and there was no doubt in my mind that it carried; the television replays later verified this. Then Randall was trapped in front for 7 when he missed a delivery from Hogg, the score then being only 46. Randall just didn't want to go. He stood there, looking up the wicket, back to his stumps, up the wicket again, and finally around the field. The umpire meanwhile had raised his finger and everybody was gathering around Hogg. Randall took a couple of minutes to dawdle off the field, and he left no doubt that he didn't fancy the decision. Fair dinkum, he was absolutely plumb l.b.w.

The two episodes left a bad taste in our mouths because they questioned the ideals of sportsmanship. Randall's situation was particularly annoying (especially after that Fourth Test), and I was pleased to read later that he had been wrapped over the knuckles by the England management for his unwarranted delay in leaving the ground.

The following day Brearley and Gooch pressed on relentlessly. They took the score past 100 before we finally broke the partnership of 69 when Brearley fell to Higgs for 46. He edged a slips catch after sticking at the crease for 203 minutes and building a solid foundation for his free-striking batsmen to follow. Gooch and David Gower then set about our bowlers in the heat and played many fine shots. Gooch had not enjoyed a good tour, but he struck the ball extremely hard in this innings and showed he can be a ruthless player. During his innings, when he was 27, one of the most unusual incidents occurred. He cut a delivery from Yardley and headed down the wicket for 2 runs. As he was on the way down the track, Kevin Wright noticed one of the bails on the ground and drew the umpire's attention to it. Then he alerted me and I appealed. But the umpire hadn't seen the bail removed, Wright and I hadn't seen it, and Gooch was as surprised as any of us. So, naturally, he was not out. It was just one of those strange things that happen, and there was no hard feelings towards Gooch about the off-bail incident. It would have been an important breakthrough at the time, as he was just getting into stride in an innings of 74. He hit seven boundaries and a six in that stay of 149 minutes, and carried the score to 182 before he was the fourth man out. His partnership with Gower realized 67 runs in an hour and, as Botham joined Gower, we looked in for a gruelling afternoon in the field. Fortunately, a deluge hit the ground at tea and washed out the last session, leaving England on 4–216 and a lead of only 18 runs.

I had the second new ball available after only seven overs on the third morning, but Jim Higgs gained considerable spin and I decided to leave it in abeyance after an early breakthrough. Botham was looking to hit the spinners out of the attack and, when he turned his attention to Bruce Yardley, he clubbed an off-drive head high to Phil Carlson. It was not a good shot from Botham, as the new ball was around the corner, and I was delighted to see the back of him after he and Gower put together a 51-run partnership in even time. Higgs meanwhile had Gower probing nervously and, although Gower's half-century came from only eighty-two deliveries, he didn't look comfortable at all against Higgs' varied deliveries. Finally, he was in two minds about playing forward or backwards, and he edged Wright a catch after contributing 65 runs in a score of 247.

We had the chance then to rip through the rest of the order with the second new ball; but our only other pre-lunch success was the scalp of Geoff Miller, who was trapped in front for 18 when he couldn't put his bat to a fast inswinger from Hurst. We showed a lot of fight in that session, because we captured three wickets while England managed only 54 runs. Hurst bounced back after the interval to remove Emburey for a duck with an outswinger that squirted to Andy Hilditch in third slip, and England's hopes of a mammoth score were shattered.

But Bob Taylor played with the commonsense and solidarity he showed in Adelaide and, with Bob Willis merely planting his large, long leg down the wicket to smother Higgs' spin, the pair carried the tally past 300. Higgs, who bowled magnificently, finally reaped his rewards with the wicket of Willis for 10 after an hour of frustrating defence. Willis edged numerous deliveries just short of the slips fieldsmen, and played and missed so many times that in desperation Jim went around the wicket to him to try a different angle. The ploy was immediately successful as Willis tried to sweep and lost his leg stump when the ball turned at right angles out of the bowlers' footmarks. Yardley then held a return catch from Hendrick before he contributed to the total; and, with Taylor unconquered on 36, the innings was complete at 308. That total took 103 overs to amass and, although it represented a most useful lead of 110, I felt we escaped lightly. The wicket was magnificent during the early part of their innings when the top oatsmen were at the crease, and had they applied the pressure with a more positive batting display they could have scored many more runs. Our bowlers, however, deserved full credit for the spirit and effort they applied in trying circumstances. Higgs captured 4-69 from thirty overs and deserved better, while Hurst also regularly beat the bat without success to finish with 3-58 from twenty overs. They were economical and penetrating bowlers and, with any sort of luck, they could have put the skids under the batsmen. That wasn't to be. Instead, we were soon on skid row ourselves, as we crumbled yet again to the spinners.

The start of our innings saw the sensational dismissal of Andy Hilditch. Poor Andy; he edged a delivery from Mike Hendrick and looked back to see it travel towards wicketkeeper Bob Taylor. There was no way that the ball carried, and in fact it was well on its way up again as Taylor grabbed it. All the Englishmen appealed, and Andy was given out. He pointed to the ground – à la Boycott – but to no avail. I watched the replay on the television set from every angle and, honestly, you couldn't believe it. The umpire must have had an extraordinary lapse of concentration to fall for that dismissal, or he couldn't have been looking. This was rather distressing, especially as we had been on the receiving end of these questionable decisions all summer.

I was also amazed that none of the English fieldsmen queried the 'catch'. Surely somebody must have seen it? Our whole team was upset about this dismissal, and feeling between the teams wasn't too pleasant as a result. Thankfully, this was the last Test, because relationships were rather strained after such a dismissal.

Anyway, we were in the hot seat once again at 1–8 and plunging headlong into another disaster. Kim Hughes went in, and almost immediately the spinners were operating. He was the victim of an Emburey delivery outside the off-stump that jumped from a good length, hit him on the glove, and ballooned to Gooch at silly short-leg. Kim was out of action for 7 with the score on 28, and Graeme Wood and I added a further 20 before the real nightmare began. Wood was batting well at this point and had no need to hurry, but he tried to loft a drive from Miller and succeeded only in presenting Willis with a catch at mid-off. That innings was wasted because he was striking the ball so well that risky shots, especially in the circumstances, were not necessary. Once Wood left, for 29, we lost two further wickets without addition to the score. Peter Toohey and Phil Carlson both failed to score as they lasted four minutes between them. Each prodded forward nervously, and gave easy leg-trap catches from the bowling of Embury. We were history. Only Bruce Yardley and I remained and, with more than two days to play and a deficit of 62, we needed to reverse the trend in miraculous fashion or pray for a flood.

Yardley immediately jumped into the spinners with gusto. He absolutely charged down the wicket – I thought he was going to stand on my toes a couple of times – and swung wildly but sensibly.

With six men hovering around the bat he had plenty of open space to find, and he scooted along to 16 in half an hour while I defended grimly to stumps for 13. The rest day wasn't much fun. We were 5–70 and forty runs in arrears, and that ate away at me for most of the day. We had simply thrown this one away, having had first use of a magnificent batting wicket only to fail and then to be caught out when the wicket was falling apart.

I was the first to go the next day as I moved down the wicket to Geoff Miller to try to smother his spin. I edged the ball and, before I could swing around, Bob Taylor had the bails off too. I was officially out caught, but I couldn't complain about that decision. So, after 110 minutes at the crease, I scored only 17 and all we could do then was hope to force England to bat again. At 6–82 that didn't even seem a reality. But Yardley continued his 'charge and attack' policy with great results, and he ensured that England batted again. Wright stuck with him well for almost an hour and, after a 32-run partnership in fifty-four minutes, they were starting to make the field spread a fraction. But Wright swept a delivery from Miller with the total on 114 and, although he hit it in the middle of the bat and with plenty of power, it travelled directly to Boycott who held the chance. Hogg was then bowled by Miller for 7, Higgs trapped at leg for 2 by Emburey, and Hurst caught and bowled by Miller for 4 to end the innings. Yardley remained unconquered on 61 after 161 minutes, and his innings was the only saving grace in our dismal innings of 143.

Miller totally destroyed us with 5–44 from 27·1 overs, and he captured 4–28 from 15·1 overs on this fourth morning. With John Emburey (4–52), the English spinners captured nine wickets for 96 between them to demolish us as they had in the second innings of the Fourth Test. I don't rate either of these spinners in the same class as the Indians – Bedi, Prasanna, and Chandra – and it is amazing the success they had. Admittedly, they had a paradise wicket to utilize as the ball spun at right angles and jumped nastily at times; and, with a cluster of men around the bat for any edges, results were guaranteed. Our batsmen played right into their hands, anchoring themselves to the crease and playing with the bat in front of the pad. The Englishmen, who play against this type of spin all the time, have mastered the art of putting the pad down the wicket and hiding the bat behind it.

Ian Botham is an expert at it. He throws his leg down the wicket and pretends he is playing a defensive shot. In fact, he is merely hiding his bat behind his pad. The ball hits him on the pad in line with the stumps but he is given not out because the umpire obviously feels he is making some attempt to play a shot. I don't object to that ploy if the umpires are going to consistently give it not out, but I do object to our batsmen not learning the same tactic. Instead of playing forward with the bat exposed – in other words inviting a bat-pad catch – they should be 'mocking' a defensive shot as Botham and most of the Englishmen do. After our collapses against the spinners this series – and especially with a tour of India coming up – I asked for a coaching clinic to be organized after the Pakistan tour here. The Board agreed and I hope that intensive training in playing spin bowling and other facets of the game will dramatically improve our playing standards.

I have always liked playing spin bowling, and I think it now comes naturally to me. Being a left-hander helps, because the off-spinner becomes a slow turning leggie and must bowl on my off-stump to have any chance of trapping me. Often I can pad the ball away if the direction is not good, or if he strays on to the leg-stump I can get down the track without too much worry and hit him straight. I feel a lot of our batsmen have been brought up on speed, speed, and more speed, and haven't really developed the skills to play spin bowling. The art of spin is returning to the scene now and, until our middle-order batsmen learn to handle the spinners, we will be vulnerable.

England needed only 34 runs to wrap up the Test and the series, but there was a minor squabble when they took the field. I wanted to start the innings with Higgs and Yardley, and so I asked the umpires for an old ball. Mike Brearley objected to this, but the umpires gave me an old ball and we went through the motions. The whole episode lasted only forty minutes and our only success was the wicket of Boycott for 13 when he mis-hit a cut and skied a catch to Kim Hughes from Higgs. So England won the final encounter by nine wickets, the series 5–1, and held the Ashes by a record margin.

I couldn't really raise a smile when I was named man-of-the-match for my first innings 121, because all the work of the summer, once condensed into a statistical margin, was hard to swallow at 5–1. Still, the summer wasn't all bad from a personal viewpoint. I had a century on my debut as Test skipper again England in Brisbane, a man-of-the-match award, the knowledge that I was the only player in the series to score two centuries, the one-day Cup series win behind me, and a Test victory in Melbourne.

Against that so much weighed heavily on my mind. Sure, we won the one-day Cup, but that is not the real thing in a summer of Australia-England clashes. The Ashes are what the battle is all about, and we simply didn't show the grit and determination in the Tests as we did in the one-day ventures. And why, if I scored two centuries, Kim Hughes one, and Graeme Wood one, did our batsmen rarely get it together to construct a formidable total that would make the tourists buckle? How could Hogg take forty-one wickets, Hurst twenty-five, and Higgs nineteen, and still we could win only one Test?

Much work was needed in the couple of weeks before the arrival of the Pakistanis, and no time in which to do it. There were Shield matches of vital importance to be played, and another four weeks of gruelling campaign before a breather. I was mentally and physically exhausted at this stage, disappointed but not without hopes of a revival. Mike Brearley and his troupe left Australia with the spoils, and congratulations to them. They were a professional and talented troupe, overall, with a couple of top notch players, plenty of average players, and a few hangers-on. Gower, Randall, Botham, Hendrick, Willis and Taylor were the pick of the crop, while Miller and Emburey also played their part. Brearley as captain won accolades from many for his performance. I have made my feelings known about that already.

10 Slaughtered

Feelings were at boiling point from go to whoa in the first showdown in this country between the Test team and a side riddled with World Series cricketers. The brief tour by Pakistan with eight WSC contract players amongst them was stacked with on-field dramas, off-field mud-slinging, and a general no-holds-barred battle between the two teams representing the rival camps. On the surface we may have been playing Pakistan as a country, but even before a ball was bowled a few people left no doubts that in effect we were pitting our skills against WSC.

No sooner had the Pakistanis arrived than the fur started flying. Asif Iqbal, one of WSC's cricket leaders, took it upon himself to label the recently completed Ashes series as a contest between 'two very mediocre teams'. As the touring team vice-captain, I can assume he wasn't speaking as a representative of the Pakistan team. This was nothing more than a pro-Packer publicity stunt, in my opinion. He went on to offer his thoughts that a compromise was the only way for the Australian team to regain its status in international ranks in a hurry. Fair dinkum, who asked him for his words of propaganda anyway? That was a nice how-do-you-do on the eve of the Test in Melbourne. From that moment there was no love lost between the two teams, particularly between the Australians and Asif.

But he hadn't finished. Even though skipper Mushtaq Mohammad apologized on behalf of the touring team for Asif's remarks during a Test eve reception – at which Asif didn't front, I might add – Asif hadn't finished his blast, or propaganda. He invited Kerry Packer into the Pakistan dressing-rooms during the Test and, although I agree that the touring party has the right to invite whomever it pleases into its rooms, I felt this was typical of his attitude.

Asif, it seemed to me, was using this tour by Pakistan only as a vehicle to push WSC. When he wasn't criticizing the Australians, giving his unsolicited views on a compromise, leaving the touring party to head to Sydney 'on business' as he did when Pakistan played in Adelaide after this Test, he was inviting the Australian Cricket Board's arch rival into the dressing-rooms of a troupe organized, paid for, and promoted by the ACB. That riled me no end, because he was making a mockery of the official visit by his country to our country. He virtually manipulated a meeting between the chiefs of the rival camps. However, full credit to ACB chairman Bob Parish and VCA president Ray Steele for inviting Kerry Packer to lunch and showing that they are men enough to extend courtesy to a media magnate, regardless of the obvious set-up organized by one of his employees.

After all this it is no wonder that feelings were carried on to the field. The story about Asif calling the Australians mediocre was pinned up in our dressing-rooms before the First Test, and that really fired up our players. When Pakistan left our shores, I felt we had shown the world that this young Australian side was ready to tackle all comers after a year's rough initiation into the international arena.

But back to the beginning. Pakistan arrived after winning one of the three Tests against New Zealand and on paper provided a formidable opposition. The touring party was:

Mushtaq Mohammad (captain), right-hand batsman and googly bowler, 55 Tests

Asif Iqbal (vice-captain), 35, right-hand batsman, 50 Tests

Anwar Khan, 24, right-hand batsman and medium-pace bowler, 1 Test

Ashraf Ali, 20, wicketkeeper, right-hand batsman, no Tests

Haroon Rashid, 25, right-hand batsman, 13 Tests

Imran Khan, 27, right-arm fast bowler, right-hand batsman, 20 Tests

Iqbal Qasim, 25, left-arm spinner, 14 Tests

Javed Miandad, 21, right-hand batsman and googly bowler, 19 Tests

Majid Khan, 32, right-hand opening batsman, 42 Tests

Mohsin Khan, 24, right-hand batsman and off-break bowler, 5 Tests

Mudasser Nazar, 22, right-hand opening batsman and
medium-pacer, 11 Tests
Sarfraz Nazar, 30, right-arm fast bowler, right-hand
batsman, 32 Tests
Sikandar Bahkt, 21, right-arm fast bowler, 12 Tests
Talat Ali, 28, right-hand opening batsman, 9 Tests
Wasim Bari, 30, wicketkeeper, 48 Tests
Zaheer Abbas, 31, right-hand batsman, 31 Tests

Of this troupe, Mushtaq, Asif, Haroon, Imran, Miandad,
Majid, Sarfraz, and Zaheer were already on the WSC
account. As this comprised the bulk of the Test team, there
was little doubt that the performances against them would
be taken as a yardstick by the public.

Pakistan's initial match against New South Wales was
rain-affected and eventually restricted to a one-day affair.
Although Pakistan won by 12 runs the lads from New
South Wales showed that the tourists were not invincible.
Meanwhile, I had the pleasure of leading Victoria to an
outright victory against Queensland to win the Sheffield
Shield. That was a great thrill.

This was only my second season as Victorian captain
and I was thrilled with the team's performance, coming
from behind early in the season to win the Shield by a convincing 16 points from Western Australia, last season's
champions. We won four games, earning 32 batting points
and 38 bowling points – and on all counts that eclipsed
each other State. Much of the credit for the win was due to
Dav Whatmore, who led the side while I was on Test duty.
So we had plenty to celebrate on that final day of the
Shield season when we were presented with the Shield.
Dav heard the news at that moment that he had earned
his Test cap; and Jim Higgs, Alan Hurst, Trevor Laughlin,
and I were also in the twelve – five Victorians! Dav's
inclusion was one of three changes made by the selectors
from the team that lost the Sixth Ashes Test to England. He
replaced New South Wales' Peter Toohey who, with only
149 runs in the series against England, was totally out of
touch. Laughlin came in into replace Phil Carlson, who had
not shown up in his two Tests with either bat or ball, and
twenty-one-year-old South Australian Peter Sleep made his

129

Test debut at the expense of Bruce Yardley. Sleep enjoyed a glory season in Shield cricket, winning the Benson & Hedges Shield player of the season award, scoring 495 runs at 35·38 and capturing 38 wickets at an average of 22·26 with his leg-breaks.

So we gathered in Melbourne for the Test and walked straight into Asif's outbursts. If that wasn't enough, Trevor Laughlin failed a fitness test two days before the match. Trevor pulled a groin muscle before the Victorian match against Tasmania a fortnight earlier and, although he played a key role in our win against Queensland to earn his Test spot, he was still obviously feeling the pinch. So on the Thursday evening before the match, he underwent a searching fitness test. Unfortunately for Trevor and the team, he injured the groin muscle again just as he was reaching top pace in the nets.

The selectors immediately conferred and flew Wayne Clark in from Perth to replace Laughlin. Clark, who was an integral part of the Test team before this summer with important contributions against India and in the West Indies, was the logical choice. His experience on the controversial Melbourne wicket promised to be a great help. But, unfortunately, Laughlin's breakdown unbalanced the team. While Clark was a more than worthy substitute as a bowler, he lacked the batting talents to completely cover Laughlin's loss. So we had a problem. Originally, I felt that Sleep would be the logical twelfth man in his first Test but, with Laughlin out, he had to come in to strengthen the batting. That, unfortunately, left only Jim Higgs as an option for the drink waiter's job. There was no choice really and, although I desperately wanted him to play, Higgs had to sit out the match.

So we went into the Test on the wrong foot yet again, while Pakistan had a full complement before coming up with this combination: Majid, Mohsin, Zaheer, Miandad, Asif, Raja, Mushtaq, Imran, Sarfraz, Bari, Sikandar, with Haroon twelfth man. That gave them an enormous amount of batting depth; three speedsters, three leg spinners in Mushy, Raja, and Miandad, and an off-spinner in Majid if required. It was a formidable combination. Fortunately, we won the first battle – I won the toss. The only hope for any assistance for the bowlers on this wicket would come on the first day, and for this reason I wanted to let Hogg and Hurst have a crack at their batsmen first. So, for the third time in seven Tests as skipper during the summer, I put the opposition in. That really was an indictment of the wickets we played on during the summer because I had no faith in them early in a match. And I suppose it reflected a lack of confidence we had in our own ability to cope with the opposition attacks.

The decision once again proved correct, however, and by mid-afternoon Pakistan was in hot water at 7–122, only to recover for a total of 196. Hogg did the initial damage, yet again, by removing both openers at a personal cost of only 5 runs. Majid Khan tried to square drive the sixth delivery of his opening over, only to edge Kevin Wright a regulation catch, and then Mohsin Khan was brilliantly snapped up right-handed by Andrew Hilditch at third slip as Mohsin tried to glide a ball through gully. Hogg then made it 3–5 and left Pakistan 3–28 when he bowled Zaheer Abbas with sheer speed after the dashing right-hander contributed only 11 runs. The crowd was right behind us and cheering every delivery. What's more, it left no doubt about its feelings towards Asif as the fans booed him all the way to the wicket. We were groaning with them when Asif edged a delivery over slips before he had scored.

But we did not have to wait long for his scalp. Hogg rested after six overs with the great figures of 3–9, and Clark was immediately successful as his replacement. Asif played back to one of his deliveries that reared sharply, and his edge was gleefully accepted by Wright. As the crowd hooted Asif all the way back to the pavilion after his innings of 9, we were on the warpath as Pakistan slumped to 4–40. Javed Miandad and Mushtaq then came together and survived many anxious moments. Finally, after a 43-run partnership, Hogg returned to split the union. Hogg was hooked for a couple of runs and then cover-driven for a boundary by Miandad, but he had his revenge when Miandad tried another drive and played the ball on to his stumps.

The normally free-striking right-hander was a subdued character in this innings of 19, as he scored from only ten deliveries in 131 minutes. We were pleased to see the back of him, as by this stage we had the backbone of the Pakistan team broken. But, as we feared, the depth of batting talent was great, and much work had to be done to wrap up the innings. Hurst chimed in with the wicket of aggressive Wasim Raja when he beat the left-hander with pace off the pitch. Raja's contribution was 13 of a 16-run union with Mushy. Imran survived a confident l.b.w. appeal from Hurst before he had scored, but then he knuckled down to give his skipper support. Mushy defied us for two and a half hours before Hurst finally accounted for him for 36. The delivery faded away slightly and Mushtaq pushed forward tentatively and gave Wright his third catch of the innings. The score was then 7–122 but we suffered at the hands of Imran and Sarfraz. Both were ruthless of anything overpitched or too short, and as our bowlers tired they made hay. Before our next break, the pair clubbed six boundaries between them in a 51-run stand in only seventy minutes. Then the end came quickly as Hurst and Wright combined again to remove Imran for 36, Peter Sleep chimed in for his first Test scalp when Sarfraz presented Wright his fifth catch of the innings, and Wasim Bari was run out without contributing. So the first day's work was a bonus for us – Pakistan all out for 196 was a fine effort on our part. Our heroes were Hogg, who finished with 4–49 from 17 overs, Hurst who returned 3–35 from 20 overs, and wicketkeeper Wright who gave yet another flawless display.

Our quest for a first-innings lead started on the wrong foot and never really looked like righting itself. It was like a pantomime of past mistakes during the summer as we were bundled out for 168 just before stumps. After so many run outs this summer I could not believe we had found a new way to end an opening stand – our openers ran into each other. I still can't believe it. Graeme Wood pulled a delivery that looked certain to reach the boundary. Both he and Andrew Hilditch were watching the outcome of the shot as they moved up the wicket when they veered towards each other, and bang! Graeme's bat caught Andrew's arm and jerked his wrist back with such force that the bat flew from his grasp. They completed 2 runs, but Wood could not even hold the bat and had to retire hurt with our total on 11. Andrew was fit enough to bat on, but he managed only 3 runs before he popped a catch to Miandad at silly square leg from a rearing Imran delivery. We were 1–11 and, with word that Wood wasn't likely to be able to bat again for at least a couple of days, virtually 2–11.

Allan Border and I then had to consolidate and, although the fight may not have been to the liking of those interested only in batsmen blasting boundaries, this was a real pressure situation. We took the score to 53, and looked on the way to balancing the ledger, when Imran bowled Allan for 20 with a ball that Allan completely misjudged and let rocket into his off-stump. Then Imran rattled my stumps for 25 and we were back in bother at 3–63. Imran, who bowls wide of the crease on most occasions, was angling the ball into the right-handers, but he had the knack of straightening the odd delivery to the left-hander and jagging it back sharply enough to take the off-stump after pitching in a position that one would normally regard as safe to allow the batsman to refrain from a shot.

He certainly fooled Allan and myself, and we learned a lesson from that experience. Now it was up to Kim Hughes and newcomer Dav Whatmore to produce the goods. And they were going well, too, as they took a more aggressive approach with hefty hitting against loose deliveries, and sharp running between the wickets. But stealing runs against the likes of Javed Miandad is always a risky business, and that eventually proved the downfall of the partnership after it yielded 34 runs. Whatmore pushed a delivery towards mid-wicket and Kim headed down the wicket for a single. But by the time he realized Dav's 'no' was serious, Miandad had swooped on the ball. His return, that broke the stumps, found Kim well short of his crease. Kim's 19 was an innings of promise cut short by yet another run out. His demise was a bitter blow, as it left two new chums at the crease and a rather lengthy tail to follow. Peter Sleep put together 10 runs in half an hour before he couldn't sway back far enough to avoid a delivery that clipped his glove and sailed through to Bari. Imran had shattered us with four crucial wickets, and he finished with

133

4-26 from 18 overs in a magnificent display of fast bowling. The end came quickly enough with Wright, Clark, and Hogg each contributing 9 runs, and Whatmore finally last man out for a valiant 43 in almost three and a half hours. Whatmore tried to lash out when Hurst departed for a duck, and Wood returned only as a token gesture to hold up an end. But he tried to work a delivery from Sarfraz to leg and was trapped in front.

Rodney Hogg was run out in exceptional circumstances, and I will have plenty to say on that in a short time. Meanwhile, we were bundled out for 168 and, with the MCG wicket now at its best for the third day, we faced an uphill task to keep in the match.

My worst fears became a reality the next day when Majid Khan and Zaheer Abbas slaughtered us with magnificent batting. The Pakistanis decided to attack from the start, and Majid and Mohsin had 30 runs on the board in better than even time before Hogg held a great return catch to dismiss Mohsin for 14. We did not look like getting another break until Hogg uprooted Zaheer's off-stump for 59 after another 135 runs were on the board. Majid played shots to all parts of the field, driving on both sides of the wicket, cutting, pulling, and lofting whenever he fancied. And Zaheer was in equally fine touch, occasionally outstripping Majid with his sheer brilliance. They increased the tempo from the time they joined forces, and their 100-run partnership took only 127 minutes. Pakistan's score raced from 100 to 150 in only forty-one minutes in the peak of the assault, and there was nothing we could do to stem the flow. As I said, the wicket invited stroke-making, and these are two of the best stroke-players in the game.

The pair completed a hat-trick of century partnerships for the second wicket by Pakistan against Australia – all of which have occurred at the MCG. Majid and Sadiq Mohammed started the ball rolling in 1972–3, Sadiq and Zaheer followed up in 1976–7, and now Majid and Zaheer completed the hat-trick. During the assault the man who was particularly on the receiving end was Peter Sleep. He had a rough initiation into international cricket as Majid gave him a fearful hammering. He was expected to come into the team as the side's Number 1 spinner, and that really was asking too much of him. He did not bowl well, giving the batsmen too many loose deliveries and, consequently, he was smashed out of the attack. Majid took eight boundaries from his opening four overs, and figures of 0–41 after four overs are not impressive in any grade of cricket.

Majid's innings of 108 included sixteen boundaries from only 156 deliveries and, by the time he lost Zaheer with the total at 165, he was only slipping into top gear. When Allan Border finally yorked him the total was 204, and Javed Miandad had aided with only a dozen runs in a 39-run partnership in forty minutes. Boy, were we pleased to see the back of Majid.

Pakistan had the ball at its feet at that stage but, to our credit, we kept plugging away and Border provided another handy breakthrough with the scalp of Miandad for 16 with the total on 209. Allan is a more than useful left-arm finger spinner and, with some expert coaching, he could develop into a very important member of our attack to complement his batting. In fact, former England spin-wizard Tony Lock has offered to coach Allan, and if a few of Tony's tricks rub off then we will be thankful. As it was, Allan forced Miandad to edge Wright a catch at the wicket, and those two quick wickets gave us breathing space for a while.

Asif and Mushtaq weren't about to let the situation slip, however, and they added 52 runs in seventy-one minutes before Peter Sleep found a grateful morsel of relief from his battering. Mushtaq, on 28, really put his weight into a pull from a short-pitched delivery and lofted the shot into the outfield. Jimmy Higgs, who was on the field substituting at the time, was at deep mid-wicket and he dived forward to hold a fantastic catch. Higgs is not renowned for his catching but this was a bobby-dazzler. As he said when we raced to him 'I never thought it was going to come down. I knew if I didn't grab it I might just as well have dug a hole and buried myself, because I wouldn't be getting another chance for Australia.'

By stumps Pakistan was 5–279, with Asif unbeaten on a score of 41 that included two sixes and three boundaries. He was obviously in top form, and the key man for us to remove on the fourth day. Rain flooded the MCG overnight, but delayed play for only an hour on the fourth day.

. Thankfully, Asif added only three runs to his overnight score before he was trapped in front by a Hogg delivery that kept low, and Pakistan's lead at that point was 327 with the tally on 6–299. Then Raja and Imran blitzed Hurst with a host of drives and pulls, and once again the tailenders had added invaluable runs. The pair added 31 in a hurry before Raja became a little too ambitious. He tried to hook a Hurst delivery that was wide outside the off-stump and edged a catch to Wright. His 28 shot Pakistan to 330, but Hurst struck again when he trapped Sarfraz in front for 1 with the total advanced only 2 runs, and only Imran really threatened to bolster the score by a great margin. He lashed out successfully for 28 runs before he tried one slog too many, when his attempted lofted straight drive lobbed safely into the hands of Wayne Clark at midwicket. Mushtaq declared at that stage with the total on 9–353, giving us the unenviable contract of scoring 382 runs for victory – we had to create a record by an Australian team in Australia to win this Test with the highest winning fourth innings tally in history.

Even so, we had fought back well to capture four wickets for 74 on this fourth day. Considering Pakistan was 2–204 at one stage, we showed a lot of fight to capture seven wickets for 149 after a fearful pounding. What we had to do now was bat sensibly and play our natural games as individuals and let the game take its course – we had plenty of time to get the runs, really, if we all chipped in together, and on this wicket a draw was definitely not out of the question. We did, however, have to shuffle the batting order and open with Dav Whatmore, because Graeme Wood's hand was still sore, but not broken, and we wanted to give him another day to recover as much as possible before he batted.

We were back in the game with a vengeance by stumps, with a score of 2–117 behind us, leaving ourselves 360 minutes to score 265 runs on the final day for an historic victory. Dav Whatmore and Andrew Hilditch shared an opening partnership of 49 and we appeared to be coasting, until Dav played a delivery from Sarfraz on to his stumps after scoring 15. That was a pity, because Dav was right behind the ball and showing signs of breaking the shackles when he gloved the ball into his stumps. Despite Dav's loss, Andrew and Allan Border played naturally and the run rate increased nicely. Andrew looked more like an opening batsman than he had in his previous innings. He had been tentative in his three previous Test innings, but this time he was positive in his actions and shaped well, prepared to play shots, and eager to take up the challenge.

He took control and reached his half-century from only 94 deliveries as he took toll of a leg-stump attack from Imran and Sarfraz. With Allan Border playing second-fiddle to a large degree, the pair put on 60 in only eighty minutes before Hilditch lost his wicket just twenty-four minutes before stumps. He tried to clip a delivery from Sarfraz to leg but missed and lost his leg stump. His innings of 62 showed the way and gave the entire team heart and confidence that the target was not beyond us, provided we batted responsibly the following day.

That bug-bear of the summer – a run out – was responsible for a disappointing beginning to our chase the final morning. This time I was the victim, the thirteenth of the summer for Australia. I was 8 at the time and Allan was about 30, when I pushed a delivery from Imran to backward square leg and called for a single. Asif was on to it like a panther and I then called 'no'. But Allan hadn't heard me, and was charging down the wicket as I looked up. There was nothing I could do but put my head down and go for my life. Asif's return beat me by half the length of the wicket.

Because of the mix-up one of us was certain to be run out and, as Allan was in fine form and looking set for a large score, I had a responsibility to make sure he was safe and only hope that Asif's throw went astray. That wasn't to be, and I was bitterly disappointed as I went back to the pavilion with the scoreboard showing Australia 3–128.

From the ruins did come a pot of gold in the form of a magnificent partnership between Allan and Kim Hughes. With intelligent running between wickets, ruthless treatment of any loose deliveries, and a common-sense approach to the task at hand, they carried us to a winning position at 3–305. They enjoyed a record fourth wicket stand of 177 against Pakistan and, with thirty minutes and the compulsory 15 overs in the last hour remaining, we were within 77 runs of a miraculous victory. This was a result of a dedicated and spirited exhibition from both players. Allan reached his maiden Test century in an innings of maturity, highlighted by powerful shots throughout his chanceless stay, especially on the leg side. At 4.30 p.m. he tried to clip a delivery from Sarfraz to leg and played the ball on to his leg stump, to depart for 105 after 373 minutes of battle.

I still cannot comprehend what followed. In 65 deliveries in fifty-five minutes, we lost seven wickets for a paltry 5 runs, including three leg byes. From an invincible position, with an historic victory there for the taking, we lost by 71 runs. Unbelievable was the only word I could find to describe it then, and I still can't come up with an alternative. Mushtaq described the win as a miracle. That's as good a description as any I guess. This is what happened:

After Allan Border departed with the score at 305, Graeme Wood joined Kim Hughes to hold up an end and let Kim continue his stylish hitting that was forging us towards victory. But he tried to cut the first delivery he faced, and edged a regulation catch to wicketkeeper Bari to be out for a first ball duck: 5–305.

Then in quick succession Peter Sleep was bowled for a duck, Wayne Clark lost his middle stump to a low delivery, and Kim Hughes made a frustrated lash that sent Mohsin a catch at mid-off when Kim was aiming for mid-wicket. Kim's exit for 84 was the end of the chase for us, and I told the players to close shop. Kim had been batting so well, but he lost sight of the goal with his indiscreet shot. We had blown our chance of victory, but with Kim there we still should have forced an honourable draw. That was a sorry end to an otherwise fine innings.

Sarfraz by this stage seemed to be unplayable. Rodney Hogg was trapped in front for a duck, and then Alan Hurst was caught at the wicket to end the most extraordinary rout I have witnessed. Kevin Wright was stranded at the other end after spending forty minutes in defiance for only 1 run.

I was shocked. Pure and simple. When I realized that Sarfraz had captured 7–1 I almost fell over. He is an honest trundler but glory, 7–1 in a Test match!! This was a freak happening, and it really took the wind out of our sails. We simply seemed to lack the experience to halt a rout during the summer. Rather than knowing how to stem the tide when the chips are down, we seem to have developed a pattern for falling apart at the seams. Even when a couple of the batsmen are really on top, their dismissal seems to trigger a collapse of monumental proportions. This was the daddy of them all for the summer.

Although I was shocked and dismayed at the outcome, I felt we had shown a lot of courage in our game. The rout hid much of the good that came out of the game from our viewpoint. The batting of Hilditch, Hughes, and Border was a bonus, and I felt that with an ounce of luck we could reverse the result in Perth.

Within a week my season was ended. While playing in a semi-final for my grade club Richmond, I tore a calf muscle and found myself on crutches. I was 28 at the time and, although I used a runner for the rest of my innings of 90 not out, I realized my chances of making the team for Perth the following weekend were slim. Despite constant treatment for the next couple of days, I had to withdraw.

That was one of the big disappointments of the summer, because I wanted to finish the season very desperately. We had shown signs of improvement in Melbourne, and I fancied that Pakistan were not unbeatable. Having gone through so much during the summer I felt empty that I couldn't see it out to the last. The only consolation was that my Victorian team-mate, Jeff Moss, finally won his Test cap at the age of 31 after a magnificent summer with the bat. Jeff topped the Shield averages and topped 750 runs for Victoria with his aggressive left-hand batting. My exit caused five changes in the team that was beaten in Melbourne, as the selectors had already dumped a third of the team. Out went opener Graeme Wood, all-rounder

Peter Sleep, paceman Wayne Clark, and twelfth man Jimmy Higgs; and in came Rick Darling, Geoff Dymock, Trevor Laughlin, and Bruce Yardley. Moss was the thirty-first new Test cap in sixteen months but, thankfully, he did have the benefit of a lot of experienced players around him. I was delighted to see the return of Rick Darling. He is a player of the future and, although he has had several setbacks during the summer, he is potentially the best opening-batsman in Australia in my opinion. And Dymock's recall was also pleasing. He bowled well all summer and really was a little unlucky to be dropped in the first place. He wasn't taking many wickets, but he was always at the batsmen, containing all the time and allowing Hogg and Hurst to have a breather for another onslaught.

I went to Perth to work on radio and television because I could not bear to miss the last game and, even though I was no longer part of the team, I felt a real grudge towards the tourists.

11   A Nasty Business

The off-field mud-slinging initiated by Pakistan paled into insignificance compared to some of the on-field dramas. Incidents in both Tests lowered the colours of cricket as we have known it, and standards of sportsmanship plummeted to unprecedented depths in the Second Test in Perth. Three incidents caused all the rumpus. Firstly, Javed Miandad began the demise when he ran out Rodney Hogg in Melbourne; after a series of mid-wicket chats, a recall, and then another 'out' decision, Hogg bashed down the stumps before departing. The Perth Test was even more dramatic. Alan Hurst ran out last man Sikandar with a 'Mankad' execution, and to top off the whole distasteful series of events, Sarfraz appealed successfully against Andrew Hilditch for handling the ball.

I was disgusted with all three events, and I am sorry that Test cricket was subjected to this type of treatment in this country. I suppose all the ill-feeling between the two sides was vented on the field, but I only hope I never play in a series where this sort of behaviour is tolerated again. Let's take a closer look at the individual incidents.

Australia was struggling for runs in the first innings in the Melbourne Test, with Hogg on 9 runs and Australia still 29 runs behind Pakistan's total. He was batting rather confidently at the time, having driven a couple of deliveries with plenty of power. Then Sarfraz bowled him a no-ball which Hogg patted gently a couple of metres from the stumps on the off-side. Satisfied that the action was ended for that delivery, Hogg strolled out of his crease and patted down a spot on the wicket.

Meanwhile Javed Miandad ran from short leg, across the pitch behind Hogg, and picked up the ball. He glanced back and, noticing Hogg out of his ground, ran several paces to remove the bails. As he did so he appealed to umpire Mick Harvey, who waited for several seconds before signalling Hogg out. Hogg was dumbfounded but took the decision on the chin and walked towards the pavilion. When he was halfway there, Mushtaq raced after him and escorted him back to the centre. Once there, umpire Harvey explained that the umpire's decision was final and, again, Hogg was ordered to leave. In frustration, he hammered two stumps out of the ground with an angry sweep of his bat.

Several points came out of this incident. Firstly, Hogg should not have left his crease when he did, and I am sure he has learned that lesson well after this incident. More importantly, Miandad's act was most unsportsmanlike. He had time enough to think what he was doing – his was not an instinctive action. He could easily have warned Hogg of his error and threatened to be more drastic if another transgression occurred. That would have been more in line with the spirit of cricket. That little run out sparked bitter feeling between the two teams. In years to come more will be remembered of the incidents in Perth. But, let's not forget that Miandad was the one who started the whole series of events.

Another aspect of the Hogg incident that should be mentioned is that a captain does not have the right to recall a batsman once the umpire has given a decision – and I must admit I was not aware of that until this match when Mushtaq tried to recall Hogg. Hopefully, that will be altered when the Laws of Cricket are revised this year, because often a captain does not have time to evaluate a situation to retract an appeal before an umpire has given a verdict. As the law stands, a captain can withdraw an appeal only, not recall a batsman.

I believe that Miandad was technically right but morally wrong in his action. Umpire Harvey had no choice but to pass judgement on an appeal. Mushtaq obviously felt that Hogg deserved another chance and that Miandad's actions were morally wrong, but by then the damage was done.

With this episode in the back of the players' minds, there was little wonder further trouble erupted in Perth. I was not competing in this game, but if I had been I would never have allowed Alan Hurst to 'Mankad' Sikandar without a warning. What happened was that Australia desperately needed to break the last-wicket partnership between Asif and Sikandar, in which Asif was palming the strike with a single from the last delivery of each over. Asif was 135 at the time and in total control, while Sikandar was miraculously making good his ground in singles that appeared to have little chance of succeeding. I have no doubts that he was backing up much too far at the end of each over, and I fancy that even if Asif played and missed he could have completed a bye before Kevin Wright could have gathered the ball behind the stumps. So, with the total on 277 and with Hurst coming in to bowl the last ball of an over after forty frustrating minutes trying to break the stand, he whipped off the bails in his bowling stride with Sikandar well and truly on his way down the track. Hurst appealed and, after a very long wait, umpire Tony Crafter raised his finger. Obviously, umpire Crafter was giving acting captain Andrew Hilditch every opportunity to withdraw the appeal in light of the Melbourne drama. But, with pressure from Hurst and no reaction from Hilditch, umpire Crafter had to be technically correct – and in my opinion morally wrong – in giving Sikandar out. Immediately, Asif, who was stunned, turned around and took an almight swing at the stumps, sending the bails flying past wicketkeeper Wright.

If both actions by Hurst and Asif were retaliation for the Melbourne showing, then that was shameful. I cannot condone running out a batsman in the 'Mankad' fashion without warning him. If he was so obviously moving out of his ground in earlier overs, the natural reaction would be to stop in mid-stride, tap him on the shoulder, and wag a finger at him to let absolutely everybody know that he was taking an unfair advantage and that next time he was up for grabs. If he did it again you could run him out without compunction. If he didn't do it again, the chances were that he would be run out attempting a suicidal single. Either way the code of ethics of the game would be preserved, and the Australian team would not have stooped to the low level set by the visitors.

As for Asif, I would just like to say that his childish act in belting down the stumps was something that we in Australia can do without. I don't want to make excuses for Hogg at the expense of Asif, but at least in Hogg's case in Melbourne there were extenuating circumstances: he was given out and was the sufferer in an unusual incident; he was recalled by the captain; and then he was totally frustrated by being given out again. In Asif's case, he did not hit the stumps in a reflex action but belted them down in disgust. That was inexcusable because, even if he objected to the situation like so many others did, he should have had the self-control to vent his objections later. His action hardly did much good for the thousands of young cricketers around this country who watched their Test stars in action. I hope that parents, cricket coaches, and school teachers impress on all young cricketers that this is just not on in any grade of cricket.

As I said, I would not have allowed Hurst's appeal to reach fruition. Instead I would have told the umpire that we were withdrawing it, and then told Sikandar in no uncertain terms that I believed he was taking an unfair advantage and that he had better be spot-on with his running from that moment on. I felt helpless, sitting in the stands, but the damage was done and there was nothing I could do about it.

But Sarfraz took the cake for downright bad sportsmanship soon after. There can be no excuses offered or accepted by Sarfraz, Mushtaq, or the Pakistan team in general for the dismissal of Andrew Hilditch for handling the ball. This disgraceful event happened when Sarfraz was bowling from the Swan River end as Australia was heading for victory. Rick Darling hit a firm off-drive to Sikandar, who was shaping to throw at the bowler's-end stumps when he saw that Hilditch was clearly safe, and content to stay that way. Sikandar dollied the ball back after feigning his throw, and the ball dribbled past the back of the stumps. Sarfraz was still three metres down the wicket, so Andy tried to be a gentleman, and picked up the ball and dollied it back towards Sarfraz.

Sarfraz avoided it like a hot potato, and instead burst forth with an appeal against Hilditch for handling the ball. Again, umpire Crafter waited an agonizingly long time, hoping that Mushtaq would come to his rescue. But, with Sarfraz almost charging him for a decision, Crafter gave Hilditch out. This time I don't even know if the decision was absolutely technically correct, but it was so morally

144

wrong that I felt shame for the grand old game of cricket.

The law covering 'handling the ball' was surely intended not to be used in such circumstances but, rather, when a player handles the ball while trying to protect his stumps or prevent his dismissal. There is, however, no grey in this law – just pure black and white. Andrew handled the ball, and so he was out. Again, I hope the revision of the Laws of Cricket sort this type of situation out, because such incidents only make a mockery of the game.

I was shocked to see Sarfraz appeal, and horrified to see Mushtaq not jump in immediately. Mushtaq should have withdrawn the appeal and spoken harshly to Sarfraz for even appealing in the first place. This was the worst showing of bad sportsmanship I have ever seen, and it could not be excused under the guise of retaliation for the earlier incident.

Andrew Hilditch has learned a very big lesson from this, and I am sure he won't be picking up a ball in any grade of cricket from now on. He erred, in that he did not read the situation correctly. Feelings were at boiling point and he should not have taken the risk of any type of dismissal – no matter how remote, or obscure. The only real satisfaction he could compensate himself with was that Australia went on to win the Test and level the series 1-all. Andrew will be a better cricketer for that experience and the fruits of victory. Cricket, hopefully, won't suffer from these indignities again. Sadly these incidents took the glamour from a spirited victory that was fully deserved after five days of fine cricket.

Australia deserved to win this Test because, from the start, it was the pacesetter. Kim Hughes, captaining Australia for the first time, kept up Australia's fine record of winning the toss when he made it seven out of eight for the summer. Not a bad effort, that. And, for the fourth time in those eight Tests, Australia put the opposition in to bat. This Perth wicket was the best of the summer and, although it promised a little help early for the pacemen, the strip made a batsman's mouth water because of its hard, shiny surface that promised pace and bounce.

Australia was away to a flying start. This time Alan

Hurst took the top billing, with a magnificent spell that spreadeagled the Pakistani top-order batsmen. Rodney Hogg provided the initial breakthrough without a run on the board, as Majid Khan glided Hilditch a fourth-slip catch in the opening over of the match. Then Hurst tore the Pakistanis apart with three wickets for 10 runs in the space of only eighteen deliveries. His first victim was opener Mudassar, who had come into the team to replace Mohsin, when the solid right-hander was caught at the wicket by Wright from a thin inside edge. He batted for forty-two minutes for his 5 runs, but he was basically playing second fiddle to Zaheer, who was in breathtaking form. Zaheer clubbed 29 runs from only 33 deliveries before he tried to hook a Hurst delivery, and Wright leapt to his limit to hold a fine catch. Pakistan was 3–41 and, a few minutes later, 4–49 as Haroon became Hurst's third victim. Haroon replaced Wasim Raja in the team following a century in Adelaide before this Test, but he was all at sea against Hurst. After edging a boundary over slips, he presented Border with a third-slip catch without another scoring shot. The decision to insert Pakistan was more than justified.

Although wickets were falling, Pakistan adopted aggressive tactics, and Asif led the way. With Hurst taking a breather, Hogg returned, only to take a fearful punishing from Asif, who hooked and drove with enormous power. Australia looked satisfied with four wickets by the final over before lunch, but they received a bonus when Asif was run out. There was no sense in the single that Asif tried to steal. He hit a Hogg delivery firmly back to the bowler and called for a single as the ball rebounded towards the off-side. Rick Darling was already on the move, and he threw down the stumps almost from side on to end a threatening innings of 35 in only forty-five minutes by Asif. He so dominated the partnership with Javed Miandad that Miandad contributed only 6 of the 41 runs.

Half the side out for only 90 runs in the opening session was a champion start, but Pakistan fought back to eventually finish with 277. That was due mainly to an unconquered 129 by Miandad, and once again solid support from the latter-order batsmen. Miandad and Mushtaq, who contributed 23 before he was also run out by Darling, added 86 in 140 minutes for the sixth wicket, and Australia then marred a golden opportunity to wrap up the innings. Miandad was twice missed in the slips by Kim Hughes while on 53 and 57, and from those escapes he never looked back. He hit drives with enormous power, cut and pulled with perfect timing and placement, and went on to be 112 not out in a score of 7–240 at stumps.

While covering the Test for radio and television from the back of the grandstand, I found a totally different view-point of proceedings. Throughout the season Australia was criticized for having the slips too close together, although on the field this did not seem to be the case. The players felt they were giving each other enough space and, when you are on ground level, you just can't tell.

But, from the elevated view, I had a completely new impression of the situation. It was obvious from there that the slips *were* too close together, therefore often hindering themselves and also not covering a wide enough arc behind the stumps. I also found that you can make a better assessment of players from a distance. I think this will be a benefit to me, because I took note of players when they were batting and bowling, and there were several aspects of particular players' games that can now be worked on in light of a distant view and a more objective assessment.

Fortunately, Australia wrapped up the Pakistan innings for the addition of only 37 more runs the following day, with the last three wickets falling for only 1 run. Alan Hurst took the bowling honours with 4–61 from 23 overs, while Dymock finally gained some results for a fine summer, finishing with 3–65 from 21·6 overs, including the last two wickets from consecutive deliveries.

Australia's challenge to overhaul Pakistan's 277 came from the top for one of the few times during the summer. In Melbourne when Australia won the Ashes Test, Graeme Wood and Rick Darling provided us with half-century partnerships in each innings, and that basically was the difference in the result of the match. Now Rick and Andrew Hilditch provided the goods and, once they set the example, Australia was always going to be near the

Pakistan total. If Australia can gain sound starts, I am sure that big scores are there for the taking, because of the amount of talent in the side. This was the case in Perth, when Rick and Andrew compiled a 96-run opening-stand. They were just 4 runs short of breaking a century opening-stand drought that has lasted twenty-five Tests since Ian Davis and Alan Turner scored 134 against Pakistan in Melbourne in 1977. And they did it with conviction, confidence, and aggression. After a whirlwind start they laid the foundation for a big first innings tally.

They blasted Imran out of the attack with 38 runs from his opening six overs, and then never looked in trouble during the middle session of play : Rick hooked and pulled with a commonsense approach, and Andy played several classy cuts and a few powerful drives. Their partnership ended shortly after tea, after 96 runs in 147 minutes, when Andrew tried to hook a delivery from Imran and his top-edge gave Zaheer a comfortable catch at first slip. Andrew's 41 was a promising follow-up to his 62 in Melbourne, and he looked a far more accomplished player in his recent innings.

Unfortunately for Australia, Rick Darling and Kim Hughes also departed before Australia finished at 3–180 at stumps. Both fell l.b.w. to Pakistan's support bowlers. After a most determined and often exciting innings of 75, Darling was trapped in front by the medium-pacer Mudassar as he aimed a big drive down the wicket. This was exactly the type of innings that makes Darling one of the most attractive and valuable players in the country, and I fancy he will be an even better player in future years. Then Kim Hughes was out for 9 when he tried to work a delivery from Sikandar to the leg just before stumps. That was a blow, because Kim is an aggressive stroke-maker who would have been ideal in a bid for quick runs on this Perth wicket.

Allan Border was the only batsman to capitalize on the position on the third day, when Australia was restricted to a 50-run lead after managing 327. Allan followed up his maiden century in Melbourne with a solid 85. He was deceived by a wrong 'un from Miandad and caught at first slip by Majid, after an innings lasting almost six hours.

This was not one of Allan's naturally free-flowing innings, but he provided the backbone to the score of more than 300 – which in itself was a milestone after an inglorious summer by our batsmen.

Jeff Moss was a bundle of nerves on his debut, and he simply could not find the middle of the bat in the first innings for 22 runs in two hours; and Dav Whatmore's innings was cut short when he gloved a rearing delivery from Imran, to be caught in the gully for 15. Actually, Alan Hurst showed the way in the finish with 16 runs in breezy fashion that boosted the lead to 50. He had followed the example of Bruce Yardley, who clubbed 19 runs in thirty-eight minutes before he was bowled by Sarfraz. All told, a 50-run lead wasn't bad, despite a magnificent start to the innings that should have ensured a larger total. However, Rodney Hogg made the evening more enjoyable when he dismissed Majid, brilliantly caught by substitute Trevor Laughlin in the gully, for his second duck of the match. Actually Majid had an extraordinary trip, scoring 1, 108, 0, and 0 in a contrast of dismal batting and one magnificent innings. By stumps, Pakistan was 1–19 and still 31 runs in arrears.

Yet again Australia had Pakistan on the run in the second innings, as Hurst and Hogg maintained the pressure with some fine bowling. Hogg struck the first blow when Zaheer edged Wright a catch after scoring 18 runs in an hour. At that stage, Pakistan was still 15 runs in the red. Then, with a credit balance of only 18, Hurst accounted for the painstaking Mudassar, after the record-holder for the slowest century in Test cricket worked for 125 minutes for 25 runs. Mudassar was the victim of a brilliant catch by Hilditch in the slips: he tried to cut and, in fact, put plenty of bat on to the shot, only to see Hilditch take a one-handed diving catch to his left.

I felt Australia could run through the opposition when first innings century-maker Miandad glanced a Hurst delivery to Wright in the same mode as Zaheer before him, and Pakistan was only 36 ahead with the tally at 4–86. Miandad's exit for 19 was a vital breakthrough. With plenty of time remaining, Australia was in the box seat. However, Asif and the hard-hitting Haroon joined forces

149

and went on the attack. They fully capitalized on the magnificent batting strip, and posted a 50-run partnership in only eighty minutes, and carried that on to 66 in 104 minutes before Haroon departed. Haroon earlier had hooked a Hurst delivery for 6, and he was on 47 when he tried a repeat dose. However, this time he hit the ball just within reach of Bruce Yardley, at forward square leg, and Yardley held an Aussie Rules mark to settle the issue. That was a telling and impressive catch, because Haroon hit the ball with the full beef of the bat, and he was shaping as a giant-killer. The total at that point was 5–152, and Yardley pressed home the advantage with the scalp of Mushtaq for 1 in the following over. Mushtaq played back to a delivery that landed on middle-stump and kept coming straight and low, and paid the penalty as he tried to work the ball to the leg side.

Pakistan was only 103 runs ahead with only four wickets in hand, but that's when Asif really asserted his authority. He moved from 28 to 101 as he completely dominated a 115-minute partnership with Imran, allowing the big-hitting team-mate only 56 deliveries. They took the score to 245 in a 92-run partnership in those 115 minutes, and Imran contributed only 15 before he tried to pull a delivery from Hurst just before stumps, and gave Wright another catch down the leg side.

The final day of the summer dawned with Pakistan 7–246. The visitors were intent on a draw and Australia was desperate for a win. Pakistan employed several time-wasting ploys, and immediately the tension was icy. Rodney Hogg gave Sarfraz a bumper blitz, and the Pakistan paceman left the field for five minutes for treatment on an elbow. It was obvious, even from the grandstand, that tempers were ready to flare. Hurst then stepped in, first to have Sarfraz caught by Yardley at backward square leg for 3, when the big Pakistani swiped at a leg-side delivery; and three balls later he removed Wasim Bari when an outside edge sailed to Dav Whatmore at first slip.

For the next thirty-nine minutes the Australians were frustrated by Asif, who expertly palmed the strike to protect Sikandar. Asif is a past-master at this, and his innings was an object lesson to any batsman wishing to

150

learn how to control a game. He simply thrashed one delivery during an over, and then squeezed a single from the final delivery to retain strike. With the total on 285, the Sikandar run out occurred to end the innings. That left Australia with 215 minutes plus 15 overs in the final hour to score 236. Victory would prevent Pakistan from its first series-win in Australia. Asif remained unconquered on 134 in an innings of five hours that included eighteen boundaries and a six. He once again proved he is one of the best players in a crisis in the world, as he has been for the past decade.

Australia's contract was difficult enough but, obviously, Pakistan had no intention of giving an inch. In thirty-five minutes before lunch they sent down only five overs, from which Rick Darling and Andrew Hilditch picked up 18 runs. The pair once again set after Imran, and carted 11 runs from his opening over of the innings.

The key to the chase was another big start from this pair, and they did not falter as they carried the score to 87 before that diabolical Sarfraz incident. Andrew had contributed 29 in that partnership, and the two-hour union kept Australia well within reach of the target, despite painfully slow over-rates by the tourists. The impressive aspect of the partnerships between Rick and Andrew was the running between wickets. There was no panic or hesitation, just total understanding and commonsense running. They forced Mushtaq to keep fieldsmen in, and enabled themselves to hit over the top. Once the fieldsmen retreated, they pushed singles at will.

When Allan Border joined Rick the tempo quickened. The score breezed past 100, and then on to 153, before Rick was brilliantly run out while attempting a second run. He turned a delivery to fine leg and was dead unlucky: Mohsin stormed in, picked up the ball at full charge in his right hand, and threw a spot-on return all in the one action. Rick's innings of 79, following his first outing of 75, was a real gem, and he set up Australia's win with his aggression. He was particularly ruthless after the Hilditch-Sarfraz incident, and he left no doubt that he personally intended to take out his anger on the Pakistanis with a series of drives and pulls that were top class. The only way for Australia to 'repay' Sarfraz and the Pakistanis, incidentally, was to win the game, and this they did with a methodical decimation of the tourists. The only other wicket to fall in the victory-bid was that of Bruce Yardley, who went to the wicket to try to put the issue beyond doubt with a brazen innings. But he too was the victim of a sensational piece of fielding from Imran. Bruce turned a delivery to fine leg and called for two runs. But Imran ran a long way, picked up the ball on the run, and his long throw hit the stumps. And he had just finished an exhausting over himself! He is a fine athlete.

The next hour and a half provided a thrilling and pleasing end to the summer. Jeff Moss joined Border, and the two left-handers clouted the Pakistani attack to all parts of the field for 81 runs in eighty-three minutes. Allan was in top form, and he again passed a half-century to continue his run-blitz against the Pakistanis, while Moss lapped up the chance to play his natural, attacking game. Moss was subdued in the first innings; but this situation, demanding aggression, was right up his alley. He really broke the spirit of the tourists when he lofted a delivery from Imran over mid-on for 6 to add to his four other boundaries in an innings of 38 not out. You could see Imran's chest deflate as that shot sailed into the members'. At that moment, I think even the Pakistanis conceded there would not be another Melbourne miracle. At the close Australia won by seven wickets, with an impressive score of 3–236. Importantly, not one Pakistan bowler boasted a wicket as 'handled ball', and two run outs accounted for the three dismissals.

In any terms, this was a fair dinkum thrashing. It compensated for the Melbourne Test disaster, when victory was at hand only to be thrown away. Australia should have won the series 2–0, or at least 1–0 with a draw in Melbourne. Anybody who believed at the start of this miniseries that the WSC-riddled side would wallop our Test team must have been rather embarrassed at the outcome.

As the curtain closed on the summer, several players came out of this final Test with flying colours, a development that augurs well for the future. Rick Darling won the man-of-the-match award for his dual innings of 70s

152

and his two brilliant run outs; Allan Border took his tally in four innings against Pakistan to 276, at an average of 92, to wrap up a glorious summer; Alan Hurst captured 9–155 for the match to give him forty Test scalps for the summer; Andrew Hilditch emerged as a talented opening-batsman; and Kevin Wright emerged as a champion young wicketkeeper.

So the summer ended on a fine note for Australia, despite distatsteful incidents on the field that took much of the gloss from the win.

I was pleased the whole summer was ended because of the physical and mental drain on myself, and I am sure the rest of the team felt the same way. After eight Tests, a demanding Sheffield Shield programme, a one-day Cup competition, and grade cricket to boot, the domestic season of 1978–9 was unrelenting in its demands. But a few weeks' break to savour that final victory was just enough to whet the appetite for the World Cup.

Scores and Statistics

TEST AVERAGES – AUSTRALIA

BATTING

	M	Inns	NO	HS	Agg	Av	Catches
A. Border	3	6	2	60†	146	36·50	3
G. Yallop	6	12	–	121	391	32·58	3
K. Hughes	6	12	–	129	345	28·75	5
G. Wood	6	12	–	100	344	28·67	6
R. Darling	4	8	–	91	221	27·63	4
B. Yardley	4	8	1	61†	148	21·14	4
P. Toohey	5	10	1	81†	149	16·56	5
G. Cosier	2	4	–	47	52	13·00	2
J. Maclean	4	8	1	33†	79	11·29	18
K. Wright	2	4	–	29	37	9·25	7c–1s
R. Hogg	6	12	–	36	95	7·92	–
J. Higgs	5	10	4	16	46	7·67	–
P. Carlson	2	4	–	21	23	5·75	2
G. Dymock	3	6	1	11	28	5·60	–
A. Hurst	6	12	2	17†	44	4·40	1
T. Laughlin	1	2	–	5	7	3·50	2
A. Hilditch	1	2	–	3	4	2·00	2

†Denotes not out

BOWLING

	O	M	R	W	Av
R. Hogg	217·4	60	527	41	12·85
A. Hurst	204·2	44	577	25	23·08
J. Higgs	196·6	47	468	19	24·63
G. Dymock	114·1	19	269	7	38·43
P. Carlson	46	10	99	2	49·50
A. Border	31	13	50	1	50·00
B. Yardley	113·2	12	389	7	55·57
T. Laughlin	25	6	60	–	–
G. Cosier	12	3	35	–	–

BATTING

	M	Inns	NO	HS	Agg	Av	Catches
D. Gower	6	11	1	102	420	42·00	4
D. Randall	6	12	2	150	385	38·50	4
I. Botham	6	10	–	74	291	29·10	9
R. Taylor	6	10	2	97	208	26·00	18c–2s
G. Miller	6	10	–	64	234	23·40	1
G. Gooch	6	11	–	74	246	22·36	9
G. Boycott	6	12	–	77	263	21·92	4
M. Brearley	6	12	1	53	184	16·73	5
J. Lever	1	2	–	14	24	12·00	1
J. Emburey	4	7	1	42	67	11·17	6
R. Willis	6	10	2	24	88	11·00	3
M. Hendrick	5	9	4	10	34	6·80	3
P. Edmonds	1	1	–	1	1	1·00	1
C. Old	1	1	1	29†	29	–	–

† Denotes not out

BOWLING

	O	M	R	W	Av
J. Lever	15·1	2	48	5	9·60
G. Miller	177·1	54	346	23	15·04
M. Hendrick	145	30	299	19	15·74
J. Emburey	144·4	49	306	16	19·13
C. Old	26·7	2	84	4	21·00
R. Willis	140·3	23	461	20	23·05
I. Botham	158·4	25	567	23	24·65
P. Edmonds	13	2	27	–	–
G. Gooch	6	1	15	–	–
G. Boycott	1	–	6	–	–

BATTING

	M	Inns	NO	HS	Agg	Av	Catches
D. Randall	10	18	2	150	763	47·69	7
R. Tolchard	3	5	1	72	142	35·50	10
D. Gower	12	20	1	102	623	32·79	7
M. Brearley	11	21	4	116†	538	31·65	11
G. Boycott	12	23	3	90†	533	26·65	5
G. Miller	11	18	3	68†	398	26·53	35
I. Botham	9	14	–	74	361	25·79	14
G. Gooch	13	23	1	74	514	23·36	13
C. Old	6	6	2	40	81	20·25	2
R. Taylor	10	15	2	97	230	17·69	36c–6s
P. Edmonds	7	9	2	38†	115	16·43	8
C. Radley	6	9	–	60	138	15·33	2
R. Willis	10	13	4	24	115	12·78	3
J. Emburey	9	12	2	42	101	10·10	9
J. Lever	6	7	–	28	67	9·57	1
M. Hendrick	8	12	4	20	68	8·50	6
D. Bairstow	Did not play in first-class match						

† Denotes not out

BOWLING

	O	M	R	W	Av
M. Hendrick	184·4	39	399	28	14·25
G. Miller	277·1	74	607	36	16·86
J. Emburey	261·7	73	563	31	18·16
I. Botham	239·3	43	848	44	19·27
R. Willis	210·3	34	696	34	20·47
C. Old	138	24	452	21	21·52
J. Lever	118·1	18	377	13	29·00
P. Edmonds	147	34	397	11	36·09
G. Gooch	26	2	80	1	80·00
G. Boycott	3	–	11	–	–
D. Randall	2	–	9	–	–
C. Radley	1	–	4	–	–

FIRST TEST

At Brisbane. Toss: Australia. Man-of-the-match: D. Randall England won by seven wickets.

AUSTRALIA

G. Wood c Taylor b Old	7	l.b.w. Old	19
G. Cosier run out	1	b Willis	0
P. Toohey b Willis	1	l.b.w. Botham	1
G. Yallop c Gooch b Willis	7	c & b Willis	102
K. Hughes c Taylor b Botham	4	c Edmonds b Willis	129
T. Laughlin c sub (Lever) b Willis	2	l.b.w. Old	5
J. Maclean not out	33	l.b.w. Miller	15
B. Yardley c Taylor b Willis	17	c Brearley b Miller	16
R. Hogg c Taylor b Botham	36	b Botham	16
A. Hurst c Taylor b Botham	0	b Botham	0
J. Higgs b Old	1	not out	0
Extras	7	Extras	36
Total	116	Total	339

Fall: 2, 5, 14, 22, 24, 26, 53, 113, 113, 116

Fall: 0, 2, 49, 219, 228, 261, 310, 339, 339

	O	M	R	W	O	M	R	W
Willis	14	3	44	4	27·6	3	69	3
Old	9·7	1	24	2	17	1	60	2
Botham	12	1	40	3	26	5	95	3
Gooch	1	–	1	–				
Edmonds	1	1	–	–	12	1	27	–
Miller					34	12	52	2

ENGLAND

G. Boycott c Hughes b Hogg	13	run out	16
G. Gooch c Laughlin b Hogg	2	c Yardley b Hogg	2
D. Randall c Laughlin b Hurst	75	not out	74
R. Taylor l.b.w. Hurst	20		
M. Brearley c Maclean b Hogg	6	c Maclean b Yardley	13
D. Gower c Maclean b Hurst	44	not out	48
I. Botham c Maclean b Hogg	49		
G. Miller l.b.w. Hogg	27		
P. Edmonds c Maclean b Hogg	1		
C. Old not out	29		
R. Willis c Maclean b Hurst	8		
Extras	12	Extras	17
Total	286	Total (for three)	170

Fall: 2, 38, 111, 120, 120, 215,
219, 226, 266, 286

Fall: 16, 37, 74

	O	M	R	W	O	M	R	W
Hurst	27·4	6	93	4	10	4	17	–
Hogg	28	8	74	6	12·5	2	35	1
Laughlin	22	6	54	–	3	–	6	–
Yardley	7	1	34	–	13	1	41	1
Cosier	5	1	10	–	3	–	11	–
Higgs	6	2	9	–	12	1	43	–

SECOND TEST

At Perth.   Toss: Australia.   Man-of-the-match: D. Gower
England won by 166 runs.

ENGLAND

G. Boycott l.b.w. Hurst	77	l.b.w. Hogg	23
G. Gooch c Maclean b Hogg	1	l.b.w Hogg	43
D. Randall c Wood b Hogg	0	c Cosier b Yardley	45
M. Brearley c Maclean b Dymock	17	c Maclean b Hogg	0
D. Gower b Hogg	102	c Maclean b Hogg	12
I. Botham l.b.w. Hurst	11	c Wood b Yardley	30
G. Miller b Hogg	40	c Toohey b Yardley	25
R. Taylor c Hurst b Yardley	12	c Maclean b Hogg	2
J. Lever c Cosier b Hurst	14	c Maclean b Hurst	10
R. Willis c Yallop b Hogg	2	not out	3
M. Hendrick not out	7	b Dymock	1
Extras	26	Extras	14
Total	309	Total	208

Fall: 3, 3, 41, 199, 219, 224, 253, 295, 300, 309

Fall: 53, 93, 93, 135, 151, 176, 201, 206, 208, 208

	O	M	R	W	O	M	R	W
Hogg	30·5	9	65	5	17	2	57	5
Dymock	34	4	72	1	16·3	2	53	1
Hurst	26	7	70	3	17	5	43	1
Yardley	23	1	62	1	16	1	41	3
Cosier	4	2	14	–				

AUSTRALIA

G. Wood l.b.w. Lever	5	c Taylor b Lever	64
R. Darling run out	25	c Boycott b Lever	5
K. Hughes b Willis	16	c Gooch b Willis	12
G. Yallop b Willis	3	c Taylor b Hendrick	3
P. Toohey not out	81	c Talor b Hendrick	0
G. Cosier c Gooch b Willis	4	l.b.w. Miller	47
J. Maclean c Gooch b Miller	0	c Brearley b Miller	1
B. Yardley c Taylor b Henrick	12	c Botham b Lever	7
R. Hogg c Taylor b Willis	18	b Miller	0
G. Dymock b Hendrick	11	not out	6
A. Hurst c Taylor b Willis	5	b Lever	5
Extras	10	Extras	11
Total	190	Total	161

Fall: 8, 34, 38, 60, 78, 79, 100, 128, 185, 190

Fall: 8, 36, 58, 58, 141, 143, 143, 147, 151, 161

	O	M	R	W	O	M	R	W
Lever	7	–	20	1	8·1	2	28	4
Botham	11	2	46	1	11	1	54	–
Willis	18·5	5	44	5	12	1	36	1
Hendrick	14	1	39	2	8	3	11	2
Miller	16	6	31	1	7	4	21	3

THIRD TEST

At Melborne. Toss: Australia. Man-of-the-match: G. Wood Australia won by 103 runs.

AUSTRALIA

G. Wood c Emburey b Miller	100	b Botham	34
R. Darling run out	33	c Randall b Miller	21
K. Hughes c Taylor b Botham	0	c Gower b Botham	48
G. Yallop c Hendrick b Botham	41	c Taylor b Miller	16
P. Toohey c Randall b Miller	32	c Botham b Emburey	20
A. Border c Brearley b Hendrick	29	run out	0
J. Maclean b Botham	8	c Hendrick b Emburey	10
R. Hogg c Randall b Miller	0	b Botham	1
G. Dymock b Hendrick	0	c Brearley b Hendrick	6
A. Hurst b Hendrick	0	not out	0
J. Higg not out	1	stp Taylor b Emburey	0
Extras	14	Extras	11
Total	258	Total	167

Fall: 65, 65, 126, 189, 247, 250, 250, 251, 252, 258

Fall: 55, 81, 101, 136, 136, 152, 157, 167, 167, 167

	O	M	R	W	O	M	R	W
Willis	13	2	47	–	7	–	21	–
Botham	20·1	4	68	3	15	4	41	3
Hendrick	23	3	50	3	14	4	25	1
Emburey	14	1	44	–	21·1	12	30	3
Miller	19	6	35	3	14	5	39	2

ENGLAND

G. Boycott b Hogg	1	l.bw. Hurst	38
M. Brearley l.b.w. Hogg	1	c Maclean b Dymock	0
D. Randall l.b.w. Hurst	13	l.b.w. Hogg	2
G. Gooch c Border b Dymock	25	l.b.w. Hogg	40
D. Gower l.b.w. Dymock	29	l.b.w. Dymock	49
I. Botham c Darling b Higgs	22	c Maclean b Higgs	10
G. Miller b Hogg	7	c Hughes b Higgs	1
R. Taylor b Hogg	1	c Maclean b Hogg	5
J. Emburey b Hogg	0	not out	7
R. Willis c Darling b Dymock	19	c Yallop b Hogg	3
M. Hendrick not out	6	b Hogg	0
Extras	19	Extras	24
Total	143	Total	179

Fall: 2, 3, 40, 52, 81, 100, 101, 101, 120, 143

Fall: 1, 6, 71, 122, 163, 163, 167, 171, 179, 179

	O	M	R	W	O	M	R	W
Hogg	17	7	30	5	17	5	36	5
Hurst	12	2	24	1	11	1	39	1
Dymock	15·6	4	38	3	18	4	37	2
Higgs	19	9	32	1	16	2	29	2
Border					5	–	14	–

FOURTH TEST

At Sydney. Toss: England. Man-of-the-match: D. Randall
England won by 93 runs.

ENGLAND

G. Boycott c Border b Hurst	8	l.b.w. Hogg	0
M. Brearley b Hogg	17	b Border	53
D. Randall c Wood b Hurst	0	l.b.w. Hogg	150
G. Gooch c Toohey b Higgs	18	c Wood b Higgs	22
D. Gower c Maclean b Hurst	7	c Maclean b Hogg	34
I. Botham c Yallop b Hogg	59	c Wood b Higgs	6
G. Miller c Maclean b Hurst	4	l.b.w. Hogg	17
R. Taylor c Border b Higgs	10	not out	21
J. Emburey c Wood b Higgs	0	c Darling b Higgs	14
R. Willis not out	7	c Toohey b Higgs	0
M. Hendrick b Hurst	10	c Toohey b Higgs	7
Extras	12	Extras	22
Total	152	Total	346

Fall: 18, 18, 35, 51, 66, 70, 94, 98, 141, 152

Fall: 0, 111, 169, 237, 267, 292, 307, 334, 346

	O	M	R	W	O	M	R	W
Hogg	11	3	36	2	28	10	67	4
Dymock	13	1	34	–	17	4	35	–
Hurst	10·6	2	28	5	19	3	43	–
Higgs	18	4	42	3	59·6	15	148	5
Border					23	11	31	1

AUSTRALIA

G. Wood b Willis	0	run out	27
R. Darling c Botham b Miller	91	c Gooch b Hendrick	13
K. Hughes c Emburey b Willis	48	c Emburey b Miller	15
G. Yallop c Botham b Hendrick	44	c & b Hendrick	1
P. Toohey c Gooch b Botham	1	b Miller	5
A. Border not out	60	not out	45
J. Maclean l.b.w. Emburey	12	c Botham b Miller	0
R. Hogg run out	6	c Botham b Emburey	0
G. Dymock b Botham	5	b Emburey	0
J. Higgs c Botham b Hendrick	11	l.b.w. Emburey	3
A. Hurst run out	0	b Emburey	0
Extras	16	Extras	2
Total	294	Total	111

Fall: 1, 126, 178, 179, 210, 235, 245, 276, 290, 294

Fall: 38, 44, 45, 59, 74, 76, 85, 85, 105, 111

	O	M	R	W	O	M	R	W
Willis	9	2	33	2	2	–	8	–
Botham	28	3	87	2				
Hendrick	24	4	50	2	10	3	17	2
Miller	13	2	37	1	20	7	38	3
Emburey	29	10	57	1	17·2	7	46	4
Gooch	5	1	14	–				

FIFTH TEST

At Adelaide. Toss: Australia. Man-of-the-match: I. Botham
England won by 205 runs.

ENGLAND

G. Boycott c Wright b Hurst	6	c Hughes b Hurst	49
M. Brearley c Wright b Hogg	2	l.b.w. Carlson	9
D. Randall c Carlson b Hurst	4	c Yardley b Hurst	15
G. Gooch c Hughes b Hogg	1	b Carlson	18
D. Gower l.b.w. Hurst	9	l.b.w. Higgs	21
I. Botham c Wright b Higgs	74	c Yardley b Hurst	7
G. Miller l.b.w. Hogg	31	c Wright b Hurst	64
R. Taylor run out	4	c Wright b Hogg	97
J. Emburey b Higgs	4	b Hogg	42
R. Willis c Darling b Hogg	24	c Wright b Hogg	12
M. Hendrick not out	0	not out	3
Extras	10	Extras	23
Total	169	Total	360

Fall: 10, 12, 16, 18, 27, 80,
113, 136, 147, 169

Fall: 31, 57, 97, 106, 130,
132, 267, 336, 347, 360

	O	M	R	W	O	M	R	W
Hogg	10·4	1	26	4	27·6	7	59	3
Hurst	14	1	65	3	37	9	97	4
Carlson	9	1	34	–	27	6	41	2
Yardley	4	–	25	–	20	6	60	–
Higgs	3	1	9	2	28	4	75	1
Border					3	2	5	–

AUSTRALIA

R. Darling c Willis b Botham	15	b Botham	18
G. Wood c Randall b Emburey	35	run out	9
K. Hughes c Emburey b Hendrick	4	c Gower b Hendrick	46
G. Yallop b Hendrick	0	b Hendrick	36
A. Border c Taylor b Botham	11	b Willis	1
P. Carlson c Taylor b Botham	0	c Gower b Hendrick	21
B. Yardley b Botham	28	c Brearley b Willis	0
K. Wright l.b.w. Emburey	29	c Emburey b Miller	0
R. Hogg b Willis	0	b Miller	2
J. Higgs run out	16	not out	3
A. Hurst not out	17	b Willis	13
Extras	9	Extras	11
Total	164	Total	160

Fall: 5, 10, 22, 24, 72, 94, 114, 116, 133, 164

Fall: 31, 36, 115, 120, 121, 121, 124, 130, 147, 160

	O	M	R	W	O	M	R	W
Willis	11	1	55	1	12	3	41	3
Hendrick	19	1	45	2	14	6	19	3
Botham	11·4	–	42	4	14	4	37	1
Emburey	12	7	13	2	9	5	16	–
Miller					18	3	36	2

SIXTH TEST

At Sydney. Toss: Australia. Man-of-the-match: G. Yallop
England won by nine wickets.

AUSTRALIA

G. Wood c Botham b Hendrick	15	c Willis b Miller	29
A. Hilditch run out	3	c Taylor b Hendrick	1
K. Hughes c Botham b Willis	16	c Gooch b Emburey	7
G. Yallop c Gower b Botham	121	c Taylor b Miller	17
P. Toohey c Taylor b Botham	8	c Gooch b Emburey	0
P. Carlson c Gooch b Botham	2	c Botham b Emburey	0
B. Yardley b Emburey	7	not out	61
K. Wright stp Taylor b Emburey	3	c Boycott b Miller	5
R. Hogg c Emburey b Miller	9	b Miller	7
J. Higgs not out	9	c Botham b Emburey	2
A. Hurst b Botham	0	c & b Miller	4
Extras	5	Extras	10
Total	198	Total	143

Fall: 18, 19, 67, 101, 109, 116, 124, 159, 198, 198

Fall: 8, 28, 48, 48, 48, 82, 114, 130, 136, 143

	O	M	R	W	O	M	R	W
Willis	11	4	48	1	3	–	15	–
Hendrick	12	2	21	1	7	3	22	1
Botham	9·7	1	57	4				
Emburey	18	3	48	2	24	4	52	4
Miller	9	3	13	1	27·1	6	44	5
Boycott	1	–	6	–				

167

ENGLAND

G. Boycott c Hilditch b Hurst	19	c Hughes b Higgs	13
M. Brearley c Toohey b Higgs	46	not out	20
D. Randall l.b.w. Hogg	7	not out	0
G. Gooch stp Wright b Higgs	74		
D. Gower c Wright b Higgs	65		
I. Botham c Carlson b Yardley	23		
G. Miller l.b.w. Hurst	18		
R. Taylor not out	36		
J. Emburey c Hilditch b Hurst	0		
R. Willis b Higgs	10		
M. Hendrick c & b Yardley	0		
Extras	10	Extras	2
Total	308	Total (for one)	35

Fall: 37, 46, 115, 182, 233, 247, 270, 280, 306, 308

Fall: 31

	O	M	R	W	O	M	R	W
Hogg	18	6	42	1				
Hurst	20	4	58	3				
Yardley	25	2	105	2	5·2	–	21	–
Carlson	10	1	24	1				
Higgs	30	8	69	4	5	1	12	1

BATTING

	M	I	NO	HS	Agg	Av
Iqbal	2	4	1	134†	222	74·00
Miandad	2	4	1	129†	183	61·00
Zaheer	2	4	–	59	117	29·25
Majid	2	4	–	108	109	27·25
Haroon	1	2	–	47	51	25·50
Imran	2	4	–	33	90	22·50
Mushtaq	2	4	–	36	88	22·00
Raja	1	2	–	28	41	20·50
Sarfraz	2	3	–	35	66	16·50
Mudassar	1	2	–	25	30	15·00
Mohsin	1	2	–	14	28	14·00
Bari	2	4	1	8†	8	2·67
Sikandar	2	3	1	5†	5	2·50

†Denotes not out

BOWLING

	O	M	R	W	Av
Raja	8	–	34	2	17·00
Sarfraz	111·3	21	322	13	24·77
Mudassar	26·1	4	93	3	31·00
Imran	94	22	285	7	40·71
Sikandar	28	2	91	1	91·00
Miandad	4	–	20	0	–
Majid	9	1	34	0	–
Mushtaq	18	–	77	0	–

BATTING

	M	I	NO	HS	Agg	Av
A. Border	2	4	1	105	276	92·00
R. Darling	1	2	–	79	154	77·00
J. Moss	1	2	1	38†	60	60·00
K. Hughes	2	3	–	84	112	37·33
A. Hilditch	2	4	–	62	135	33·75
D. Whatmore	2	3	–	43	73	24·33
G. Yallop	1	2	–	25	33	16·50
K. Wright	2	3	1	16	26	13·00
B. Yardley	1	2	–	19	20	10·00
A. Hurst	2	3	–	16	16	5·33
P. Sleep	1	2	–	10	10	5·00
G. Wood	1	2	1	5†	5	5·00
W. Clark	1	2	–	9	9	4·50
R. Hogg	2	3	–	9	12	4·00
G. Dymock	1	1	1	5†	5	–

†Denotes not out

BOWLING

	O	M	R	W	Av
A. Hurst	87·4	11	325	15	21·67
A. Border	18	5	44	2	22·00
R. Hogg	75	13	257	10	25·70
G. Dymock	44·6	9	137	4	34·25
P. Sleep	15·7	2	78	2	39·00
B. Yardley	28	5	94	1	94·00
W. Clark	38	10	103	1	103·00

FIRST TEST

At Melbourne. Toss: Australia. Man-of-the-match: S. Nazar Pakistan won by 71 runs.

PAKISTAN

Majid c Wright b Hogg	1	b Border			108
Mohsin c Hilditch b Hogg	14	c & b Hogg			14
Zaheer b Hogg	11	b Hogg			59
Miandad b Hogg	19	c Wright b Border			16
Asif c Wright b Clark	9	l.b.w. Hogg			44
Raja b Hurst	13	c Wright b Hurst			28
Mushtaq c Wright b Hurst	36	c Higgs (sub) b Sleep			28
Imran c Wright b Hurst	33	c Clark b Hurst			28
Sarfraz c Wright b Sleep	35	l.b.w. Hurst			1
Bari run out	0	not out			8
Sikandar not out	5	did not bat			
Extras	20	Extras			19
Total	196	Total (for nine)			353

Fall: 2, 22, 28, 40, 83, 99, 122, 173, 177, 196

Fall: 30, 165, 204, 209, 261, 299, 330, 332, 353

	O	M	R	W	O	M	R	W
Hogg	17	4	49	4	19	2	75	3
Hurst	20	4	55	3	19·5	1	115	3
Clark	17	4	56	1	21	6	47	0
Sleep	7·7	2	16	1	8	0	62	1
Border					14	5	35	2

AUSTRALIA

G. Wood not out	5	c Bari b Sarfraz	0
A. Hilditch c Miandad b Imran	3	b Sarfraz	62
A. Border b Imran	20	b Sarfraz	105
G. Yallop b Imran	25	run out	8
K. Hughes run out	19	c Mohsin b Sarfraz	84
D. Whatmore l.b.w. Sarfraz	43	b Sarfraz	15
P. Sleep c Bari b Imran	10	b Sarfraz	0
K. Wright c Imran b Raja	9	not out	1
W. Clark c Mushtaq b Raja	9	b Sarfraz	0
R. Hogg run out	9	l.b.w Sarfraz	0
A. Hurst c & b Sarfraz	0	c Bari b Sarfraz	0
Extras	16	Extras	35
Total	168	Total	310

Fall: 11, 53, 63, 97, 109, 140, 152, 167, 167, 168

Fall: 49, 109, 128, 305, 306, 308, 309, 310, 310

	O	M	R	W	O	M	R	W
Imran	18	8	26	4	27	9	73	0
Sarfraz	21·6	6	39	2	35.4	7	86	9
Sikandar	10	1	29	0	7	–	29	0
Mushtaq	7	–	35	0	11	–	42	0
Raja	5	–	23	2	3	–	11	0
Majid					9	1	34	0

172

SECOND TEST

**At Perth.   Toss: Australia.   Man-of-the-Match: R. Darling
Australia won by seven wickets.**

PAKISTAN

Majid c Hilditch b Hogg	0	c sub (Laughlin) b Hogg	0
Mudassar c Wright b Hurst	5	c Hilditch b Hurst	25
Zaheer c Wright b Hurst	29	c Wright b Hogg	18
Miandad not out	129	c Wright b Hurst	19
Haroon c Border b Hurst	4	c Yardley b Dymock	47
Asif run out	35	not out	134
Mushtaq run out	23	l.b.w. Yardley	1
Imran c Wright b Dymock	14	c Wright b Hurst	15
Sarfraz c Wright b Hurst	27	c Yardley b Hurst	3
Bari c Hilditch b Dymock	0	c Whatmore b Hurst	0
Sikandar b Dymock	0	run out	0
Extras	11	Extras	23
Total	277	Total	285

Fall: 0, 27, 41, 49, 90, 176, 224,
276, 277, 277

Fall: 0, 35, 68, 86, 152, 153,
245, 263, 285

	O	M	R	W	O	M	R	W
Hogg	19	2	88	1	20	5	45	2
Hurst	23	4	61	4	24·7	2	94	5
Dymock	21·6	4	65	3	23	5	72	1
Yardley	14	2	52	0	14	3	42	1
Border					4	—	9	0

AUSTRALIA

R. Darling l.b.w. Mudassar	75	run out	79
A. Hilditch c Zaheer b Imran	41	handled ball	29
A. Border c Majid b Miandad	85	not out	66
K. Hughes l.b.w. Sikandar	9		
J. Moss c Bari b Mudassar	22	not out	38
D. Whatmore c Asif b Imran	15		
K. Wright c Bari b Mudassar	16		
B. Yardley b Sarfraz	19	run out	1
G. Dymock not out	5		
R. Hogg b Imran	3		
A. Hurst c Bari b Sarfraz	16		
Extras	21	Extras	23
Total	327	Total (for three)	236

Fall: 96, 143, 161, 219, 246, 273, 297, 301, 304, 327

Fall: 87, 153, 155

	O	M	R	W	O	M	R	W
Imran	32	5	105	3	17	1	81	0
Sarfraz	35·1	7	112	2	19	1	85	0
Sikandar	11	1	33	1				
Mudassar	16	2	48	3	10·1	2	35	0
Miandad	2	–	8	1	2	–	12	0

**Give them
the pleasure of choosing**

Book Tokens can be bought
and exchanged at most
bookshops in Great Britain
and Ireland.

NEL BESTSELLERS

T045528	THE STAND	*Stephen King*	£1.75
T046133	HOW GREEN WAS MY VALLEY	*Richard Llewellyn*	£1.00
T039560	I BOUGHT A MOUNTAIN	*Thomas Firbank*	95p
T033988	IN THE TEETH OF THE EVIDENCE	*Dorothy L. Sayers*	90p
T038149	THE CARPET BAGGERS	*Harold Robbins*	£1.50
T041719	HOW TO LIVE WITH A NEUROTIC DOG	*Stephen Baker*	75p
T040925	THE PRIZE	*Irving Wallace*	£1.65
T034755	THE CITADEL	*A. J. Cronin*	£1.10
T042189	STRANGER IN A STRANGE LAND	*Robert Heinlein*	£1.25
T037053	79 PARK AVENUE	*Harold Robbins*	£1.25
T042308	DUNE	*Frank Herbert*	£1.50
T045137	THE MOON IS A HARSH MISTRESS	*Robert Heinlein*	£1.25
T040933	THE SEVEN MINUTES	*Irving Wallace*	£1.50
T038130	THE INHERITORS	*Harold Robbins*	£1.25
T035689	RICH MAN, POOR MAN	*Irwin Shaw*	£1.50
T043991	EDGE 34: A RIDE IN THE SUN	*George G. Gilman*	75p
T037541	DEVIL'S GUARD	*Robert Elford*	£1.25
T042774	THE RATS	*James Herbert*	80p
T042340	CARRIE	*Stephen King*	80p
T042782	THE FOG	*James Herbert*	90p
T033740	THE MIXED BLESSING	*Helen Van Slyke*	£1.25
T038629	THIN AIR	*Simpson & Burger*	95p
T038602	THE APOCALYPSE	*Jeffrey Konvitz*	95p
T046850	WEB OF EVERYWHERE	*John Brunner*	85p

NEL P.O. BOX 11, FALMOUTH TR10 9EN, CORNWALL

Postage charge:

U.K. Customers. Please allow 30p for the first book plus 15p per copy for each additional book ordered to a maximum charge of £1.29 to cover the cost of postage and packing, in addition to cover price.

B.F.P.O. & Eire. Please allow 30p for the first book plus 15p per copy for the next 8 books, thereafter 6p per book, in addition to cover price.

Overseas Customers. Please allow 50p for the first book plus 15p per copy for each additional book, in addition to cover price.

Please send cheque or postal order (no currency).

Name ....

Address ....

....

Title ....

While every effort is made to keep prices steady, it is sometimes necessary to increase prices at short notice. New English Library reserve the right to show on covers and charge new retail prices which may differ from those advertised in the text or elsewhere. (3)